DAMP DOGS & RABBIT WEE

Cee Tee Jackson

DAMP DOGS & RABBIT WEE

Copyright © 2015 Cee Tee Jackson

All rights reserved.

ISBN-13:978-1515204954

ISBN-10:1515204952

CONTENTS

ACKNOWLEDGMENTS

With thanks to:

Greig Jackson for the cover artwork.

Sue Harris (author of 'The Contest') for help, support and kind words.

Members of the Harper Collins Authonomy website for their feedback:

(Andrea Grace; Rob Gregson, and Corben especially.)

Members of the Scribophile community for their enthusiasm and support:

(Loren Evantine; Victoria Jacks, and Robin Facer especially.)

The Inca Project for their patience, encouragement and guidance. (www.incaproject.co.uk)

(Robert Wingfield especially.)

My lovely, understanding wife, Diane, for putting up with my hermit-like tendencies throughout the writing of this book. And our two sons, Greig and Brett, just for being our sons.

1. THE TRIAL

The exasperated cries of "Roo, Roo – come here. Now, Roo." had been growing in intensity. It was easy to imagine a few hushed expletives being tagged onto the futile commands.

"I'm so sorry," gasped the breathless and embarrassed middle-aged woman as she appeared over the crown of the hill. A limp, unattached dog-lead dangled from her left hand. "He's got selective hearing, that one," she continued between gulps of air.

Roo, we deduced, was the name of the seemingly ownerless little Jack Russell Terrier that had befriended Cassie and Roxy.

"He's fine, don't worry," reassured my female companion, the owner of the two schnauzers we were walking. "Roxy enjoys the company – her sister, Cassie, isn't one for playing much."

As we were all headed in the same direction around the mist-enshrouded loch, we walked together, and chatted – mainly 'doggy talk,' of course.

This was my first outing as a professional dog walker. It was a 'trial' walk – the chance to prove to Cassie and Roxy's owner, an acquaintance from my tennis club, that I could handle her two energetic and strong dogs.

An hour or so earlier, it was Cassie, the older, taller and less sociable of the Schnauzers who seemed to be testing me.

Having parked my van, I crunched my way up the long, loose-chipped driveway towards the large, imposing front-door, unsure of the welcome I could expect. It didn't take long to find out.

No door-bell was needed to announce my arrival. Cassie had both seen and heard my approach and was already in full defensive mode. I watched through the glass-fronted door as Cassie threw herself down the long staircase that led towards the entrance, barking, snarling, and baring her teeth. She ran the length of the long hallway and slammed herself into the door that separated us.

With Cassie restrained by her owner, no mean feat for a petite woman in her fifties, I entered the house with considerable trepidation. After a brief introduction, I sat down on the wooden chair in the hallway. Sitting upright and with my hands on my knees, I gave the nod for Cassie to be released.

For a couple of minutes she continued her tirade of aggression in a final bid to scare off this unwanted intruder.

If I didn't win this battle of wits, then I'd have been as well shelving the whole idea of a petcare business right there and then.

I tried hard to appear calm, but my heart raced and a bead of cold sweat rose on my forehead, trickling slowly down the side of my nose, intent on telling the truth.

This now became a waiting game. I sat motionless and spoke quietly to Cassie. I reassured her that I was not a threat, but proved also that I could not be intimidated.

Before long, I gained her trust and respect. Several minutes later, both she and her sister, Roxy, happily hopped up into the crate in the back of the van, and we all headed off for their late afternoon exercise.

The walk went well. The dogs behaved impeccably; they had walked off-lead, remained close to me, and obediently responded to my recall whistle when they looked likely to stray. They also proved to be very sociable and played happily with their new little friend, Roo.

Well, Roxy played. Cassie remained haughty and aloof, but at least tolerated their hyperactive antics.

As we neared the end of the walk, I felt optimistic at the way things had panned out. I believed I'd proved myself and perhaps I'd soon sign up my first client?

Shortly before going our own ways, the three dogs were encouraged to play in the water at the loch edge. We watched as Roxy and Roo gambolled on the shore, and chased each other in and out the cold, gentle, breeze-driven waves.

Cassie looked on full of disdain. This was not her idea of fun. Fun was for the young and immature.

Suddenly, Roxy rushed out the water, her attention diverted towards a nearby gorse bush. Her owner knew what was about to follow.

"Roxy. Come back here. Now!" she yelled, a hint of panic rising in her voice.

She frantically called for Roxy to return, which she duly did a few seconds later – but with a rabbit kit writhing in her jaws, its back legs limp and broken.

Roxy ran into the water choosing to ignore her owner's frantic instruction to "DROP." The poor little kit, still alive, but barely, was discarded into the loch and left to flounder.

By now, even Cassie barked with excitement as she realised there was fun to be had in the water after all. Roo's yelps had developed an even higher pitch and his stubby little tail wagged back and forth like an unhinged rudder as he too ran back into the loch.

Splashing in the water, around the distressed young rabbit, the dogs' frenzied barking seemed tantamount to cruel gloating.

With their normally obeyed recall commands being totally blanked, the two owners were now bordering distraught, their voices ever more desperate. Even the promise of "biscuits for good girls," fell upon unaccepting ears. It was chaotic.

Very quickly, it became apparent that the only movement being made by the young rabbit was that encouraged by the motion of the small waves on the loch. The poor little kit had met its untimely end.

With the excitement of the chase and the challenge of the kill now spent, the three dogs soon lost interest and we eventually managed to coax them out the water.

Surely it was never meant to be like this? Here was I, on my first outing as a Pet Professional, and I had just witnessed a young animal lose its life. I adopted a philosophical approach, however, and reassured myself that this was simply the way Nature worked.

We rounded up the dogs to head back to the van. Cassie and Roxy obediently, and somewhat sheepishly, returned to be hooked back on their leads.

The little Jack Russell? He had found some fox scat and was making the most of the confusion by thrashing around in it, covering the whole of his back in the pungent mess.

I looked on aghast.

"I don't know what's got into them today?!" exclaimed the smelly one's owner. "It's not usually as mad as this."

As I was to later discover, she lied.

*****

2. THE VERDICT

You could say that I chose to enter the petcare profession through a love of animals and a long-standing interest in animal behaviour. You could, however, also say that it was through a love of having food to eat and the requirement to pay a monthly mortgage.

My entire working life, twenty-eight years, had been spent with Bank of Scotland. I had fully committed my career to them, attaining full Institute of Banking (Scotland) qualifications, moving house several times and working many, many hours of unpaid overtime. I'd worked my way from office junior to Branch Manager, via spells in International Division and Business Banking.

In October 2004 though, I was unceremoniously forced into voluntary redundancy. I often wonder if it was anything to do with the fact that I was rather outspoken about the tactics for selling Payment Protection Insurance.

Actually, I was quite outspoken about all aspects of the new trendy banking culture. The honest principles of making money through providing a service and helping people were being usurped by an unnecessary greed and focus on selling rather than banking.

Whatever the reasons, suddenly I was an ex-bank manager.

Still – 'every cloud,' and all that. I had a plan.

My ex-neighbour and closest friend, was looking to expand his lighting distribution business and was keen to have me on board with a view to running the office. It was a very small business and I would bring the numbers up to three. At the time though, considering the ambitions and prospects, it made sense that I invest in a director's stake.

My plan, however, transpired not to be very good. In fact it was a bit of a disastrous one.

It seems my supposed best friend had seen in me not so much someone who could enhance his business, but a ready-made cash-cow bearing a healthy redundancy cheque.

By the anniversary of my joining, I could see a very real potential for the business failing. I made my concerns known. Regrettably it seems my banking experience and pragmatism was regarded simply as negativity.

I took a voluntary pay-cut of twenty per cent to help keep the company liquid, but my lead was not reciprocated.

Tensions built and a few months later, I was jobless again.

This time though, there was no pay-off. There was no phone-call that evening from my 'friend' (now in inverted commas) to express his sorrow at the way things had turned out. There was no proposal for returning my investment. It cost me fifteen hundred pounds in lawyers' fees to force the issue – and even then it took many months for repayment to be made in full.

This was even harder to take than the first redundancy. I really felt I'd been taken for a mug, and by someone I had trusted. I'd been betrayed by this charlatan. I was angry. More than angry: as we say in these parts, I wouldn't have pissed on this bloke if he was on fire!

The passage of time, however, has seen my stance mellow somewhat.

I now reckon I would have pissed on him - but maybe not quite enough to put the fire out.

The following ten months were spent job-hunting. My remaining funds were simply spent.

Ironically, I was told at a couple of job interviews, I was too qualified for a return to branch banking. The Royal Bank of Scotland did say I 'showed potential,' for the more junior position of Deposits Manager, and that I should re-apply six months down the line.

I laughed.

I laughed even louder when it was announced that the Chief Executive who took that very bank to the brink of oblivion, had precisely no banking qualifications.

My smug mirth soon, however, turned to concern. I didn't want to think about downsizing the family home, but it was fast becoming the only option.

Then, in a moment of pure chance, I spotted a franchise opportunity for a pet care business.

The notion of a pet care business was appealing. The idea of paying away a percentage of my monthly takings to a franchisor, less so.

Throughout my years in banking, I had witnessed the set-up of many small businesses. The majority flourished. Some of course struggled and a small number unfortunately failed. I reckoned I'd amassed sufficient knowledge to go it alone.

Walking dogs, feeding cats, boarding rabbits and guinea pigs – how hard could it be?

The idea of employing a dog-walker was still a novel one in Scotland. To attract business, I needed to present a professional and trusted image.

Adverts were paid for in the local advertising magazine that reached fifteen thousand households every month. Bespoke, branded polo shirts, fleece jackets and caps were ordered.

The recently acquired white van was decorated with decals of the business logo and contact numbers. The van was often intentionally parked in prominent spaces close to the entrance of the various supermarkets. I'd also park next to popular dog-walking routes in the area, and chat to anyone passing. Glossy leaflets were given to anyone I saw with a dog. I set up a stall at the local agricultural fair and likewise, at the village church's Spring Fayre.

I also bought a set of highlighter pens. I was taking this business very seriously.

By May 2007, I was raring to go. The spare room was converted into an office. It became the 'nerve centre,' although as the first few weeks passed without any concrete bookings, it was soon re-christened the 'nervous centre.' I seemed to spend endless hours in there just waiting for the phone to ring, needlessly re-arranging as-yet-empty files and listening to loud punk music.

Two weeks after my trial walk with Cassie and Roxy, the phone rang.

Could I take them for a walk the following Monday afternoon?

I'd passed the test. I was in business.

I was a 'Dog Walker.'

Or as the inner snob in me prefers, a Pet Professional..

*****

3. THE BUSINESS

The initial years were not easy. There was no chance of taking a holiday for a start. Every day was a working day – including Christmas and New Year's Day. No booking could be turned away until a regular client base had been established.

The closest I got to a vacation, was taking a small angler's stool with me when walking by the local river on hot, sunny days. While the dogs played in the water, I'd sit down and momentarily close my eyes. I'd listen to the kids happily splashing around upstream, and imagine myself on some exotic, sun-drenched beach, far, far away.

But this is West of Scotland. There's not much in the way of sunny days here. It was neither a long-lasting nor convincing dream.

Consequently, I would sometimes sit in the van with both the heater and CD player turned up full, and blast out some reggae, ska or soca sounds.

I'd then open the tube of sun cream that lies, more in hope than expectation, in the glove compartment. I'd smear a little above my top lip, which meant that each time I took a deep breath, the coconut infused aroma would waft me to a Caribbean island.

For a minute or so, at least.

Although I count myself very lucky, health wise, injuries and illness were, and still are, a nightmare.

I've not lost a day through ill-health since starting the business eight years ago, although there have definitely been some when I would have been better advised to stay home.

However, since there's no pay if I don't work, I have, over the years, walked dogs and crawled into chicken runs whilst suffering from: cracked ribs; pulled hamstrings; pulled calf muscles; flu – the proper, non-man-flu strain, really, and even labyrinthitis.

Not all at the same time, I'm pleased to say.

But aside from the financial implications of not working, there's also that instilled sense of customer expectation that over-rides my discomfort.

If there was one thing I took from serving all those years in Branch Banking, it was that a good, solid business is based on the sturdy foundation of excellent customer service. I'd like to think that someday the banking industry will return to this way of thinking.

But for the time being, I'll carry the torch.

Dog-walking as a job may be viewed by some as nothing much more than an extra pocket money earner; a chance to fill some otherwise boring hours at home and make a little casual cash on the side.

For me though, it was always going to be my principal source of earnings, and so it was important I adopted a professional approach from the start.

Yeah – 'Pet Professional.' That has a nice ring to it.

OK – the core of my business is dog walking. So I'm a 'dog walker,' pure and simple, in the eyes of most clients. I get it. It's understandable and no doubt I'll always be referred to as just that.

It's like parents meeting at the school gates to ferry their kids home. In much the same way as they quickly become known as 'Greig's mum,' or 'Brett's dad,' so I became known as 'The Dog Walker.'

Perhaps I should have regarded it as a compliment. There were no other dog walkers in the immediate area and use of the word 'the' implied a uniqueness.

However, it wasn't too long before I was being introduced to guests at various parties and functions as 'my,' dog walker. It seemed that not only had I lost my personal identity, but I was now regarded as a chattel. And worse – I was no longer 'the' dog walker. There were others.

I didn't mind really. So long as people were talking about me in positive terms with regard to my business, it could only be good.

I was a little concerned however that the term 'dog walker,' didn't convey the range of services I planned to offer. For instance, would a prospective client contact a 'dog walker' to look after their pet tarantula?

I'm not big on spiders or bugs in general, so thankfully, nobody has yet approached me to care for a large, hairy arachnid. However, one of the early jobs I was given was to look after a bearded dragon and two geckos.

Their daily diet consisted of live crickets and hoppers – little mini locust- type insects. That was the first test of my desired 'professional,' approach to my work.

I felt comfortable with the reptiles. I enjoyed watching them and handling them. But feeding them live food? At that moment, I would rather have been dealing with a rabid dog.

I don't understand why harmless little insects should fill me with dread. I've never liked them it's true, but I don't like tomatoes, or kiwi fruit for that matter. I don't feel threatened by either of them.

Brian, the bearded dragon looked up at me, his eyes following my every movement.

"Get on with it, pal. Starving lizard down here – come on, they're hardly gong to bite your fingers off. I might, though, if you don't get a move on. Sort it out, man."

With great trepidation, I tentatively, but also rather clumsily, opened the transparent container in which about thirty hoppers were anxiously awaiting their fate. This was the opportunity the escape committee were waiting for. Four or five took their chance and jumped out onto the carpet below.

Quickly, I slammed the container shut.

Brian closed his eyes briefly, and turned his head. I could sense him exhaling an incredulous sigh as I scurried around the bedroom floor, hunting the escapees.

I succeeded in tracking down three. The others that made it over the wall of the plastic carton went on their way with my blessing. I knew they wouldn't survive, but at least they had bought themselves more time.

I took a deep breath and gently as I could, caught the three absconders in the tweezers provided by the pets' owner.

The first little insect struggled in the grip of the two metal prongs, I felt a totally unexpected compassion for this tiny creature whose life I was about to end in the jaws of an avaricious lizard. Feeling a tad guilty, I dropped it, followed by the two others, into the vivarium.

I watched in stupefied amazement as the bearded dragon devoured the first of the hoppers, then set about stalking his second and third course.

My stomach turned somersaults. This queasiness was not, however, brought on by watching Brian at breakfast. It was because for the first time in my adult life, I had sentenced a living creature to death.

OK – strictly speaking, it was the second time. But the rabbit kit wasn't all my doing.

*****

4.   THE MESS

What struck me most in the early days of my new profession, was the sheer amount, and various forms, of bodily waste that had to be cleared.

If you own a dog, you'll likely have to pick up once a day - maybe twice if there's plenty of roughage in the diet. Perhaps you keep rabbits or guinea pigs and clean their hutches once a day – you may even get away with once every few days. You have a horse? Muck out once a day.

A cat owner? Aren't you the lucky one? It's your neighbour's problem, next time they weed the garden.

But, a Pet Professional? Walking up to twenty-two dogs a day, looking after two hutches of small animals and possibly undertaking two, twice-daily cat visits? Then you'd best find a poo-bag or nappy sack supplier and open a credit account. You're going to need shed-loads of the things.

When I first started out, I was the only Pet Professional in the area. There are now in excess of ten. Consequently, there are many more dogs being walked at the same time in the park and local residents are quick to complain about the amount of dirt left lying around.

Of course, it would be simple enough to add this to the long list of accusations against investment bankers. They probably wouldn't even notice. They'd likely just make some glib, standardised apology and pay a hefty fine before continuing to do what they do best.

But then in their defence, the mess they generally leave behind doesn't smell and is not likely to carry harmful bacteria.

The blame therefore invariably falls upon the local professional dog walkers for not cleaning up after their charges. Perhaps, in some cases, this may be justified.

Not me, though, Oh no, no, no.

Never would I have considered that carrying a few bags of dog-poo would fill me with such a sense of self-righteousness. I stride through that park every day, whistling a happy tune, six dogs in tow, and my bulging, pink, nappy sacks proudly displayed as if they were Versace handbags.

There are times though when mere nappy sacks are completely inadequate. Times when industrial cleaners would be a better option.

Some days walking into a client's house, I'll come face to face, or maybe that should be face to faeces, with a wall of smell. Usually, these visits are first thing in the morning and really not what you'd want on top of a greasy bacon roll and strong black coffee.

In the main though, cats are good at using their litter trays. There are however occasions where the poor wee things are suffering physical or even psychological problems that result in 'out of box,' experiences. Little foul-smelling and often squidgy piles lurk behind settees, under beds and quite frequently beside the door to the garden. Bless!

Generally, this happens in houses without cat-flaps.

Conversely, in those that are fitted with them, an array of dismembered or possibly still living, mice and birds are dragged into the house and strewn across the floor. Even if there is more than one cat in the household, it's normally quite easy to spot the culprit from the proud, but slightly coy expression on the guilty party's face.

Such messy incidents are not confined to indoors either. Not so long ago, Buddy, a cute little white, Japanese spitz dog, rolled in some foul smelling mess he found in a field. I took him to the nearby ford and encouraged him to go for a swim. On his return to shore, though, I unfortunately stood too close as he shook himself dry, and was showered with a diluted but still intensely pongy solution.

It didn't end there.

An hour later, whilst on an off-lead walk with two Welsh springer spaniels, there was a sudden rustle of leaves at the edge of the country lane. Oscar and Rowan came to an immediate halt. Their heads cocked to one side, they were trying to pinpoint the source of the disturbance in the undergrowth, when an impatient grey squirrel made a very bad judgement call.

Rather than wait a few seconds until we had passed by, it decided to scurry across our path. It was the last decision it would ever make. It bolted from the base of a rhododendron bush, straight into the close gaze of Oscar, the younger and more exuberant of the two dogs.

Oscar pounced, and within seconds had shaken the squirrel almost to death. I managed to prise the screaming little rodent from his jaws, but sadly, within a few seconds the squirrel had become carrion for the crows.

In the course of the failed rescue mission, I was liberally splashed with blood. This mingled not so beautifully with the pre-existing stench of god-knows-what Buddy had transferred onto my clothes. I was stinking.

A short while later, en route to returning Oscar and Rowan to their owner, I had a meeting with a prospective client at their home.

"Hello. You must be Cee Tee," greeted the elegant woman on the doorstep of her rather plush looking house. "In you come. Take a seat, please," she said.

"If it's all right with you, I think it's probably best if I stand."

*****

5. THE MISCHIEF

From their sometimes petty little idiosyncrasies to their natural enthusiasm and yearning for fun, it never ceases to amaze me how much dogs and young children are alike. And let's not forget their propensity for making mischief.

Take Marley, for example. He's a lovely, seven years old English springer spaniel. I've been lucky enough to have walked with him on a daily basis ever since he was a puppy. Even then, he was the embodiment of those childlike characteristics.

He's full of life, obedient and completely non-confrontational with other dogs. That is, when out in the open air, during a walk.

But each day, just before we travel by van to the start of the walk, Marley's personality morphs from a canine Dr Jekyll to a doggie Mr Hyde.

When we started walking together, Marley had the dog-crate to himself. The business has grown since then and that particular time-slot became the most popular. Consequently, for some time now, Marley has been required to share space in the crate with other members of the pack. And he's not happy with this arrangement.

All the dogs know Marley, some of them for many years. They've all walked with him before, and shared the crate, so know what to expect.

'Anything for a quiet life,' seems to be the maxim. For most, the simplest option is to avert eye contact and cower as close to the floor as possible.

Apart from Bramble.

Bramble is a three year old Kerry blue / schnauzer cross bitch, about a third the size of Marley. The first time they were placed together in the crate, she received the expected treatment. Marley's top lip lifted and he bared his teeth. He barked incessantly, towered over her in domineering fashion and growled in her face.

However, also for the first time, he met with a dog who would not accept his bullying, and she snapped at him, resulting in a rather pathetic whimper from the bold Marley.

Next day, Marley reverted to type and ran out from his house to the car, snarling aggressively as usual. Without checking who was already in the crate, he jumped in, prepared to give the occupants a hard time. Mid-jump and mid-bark though, he recognised Bramble. He promptly averted his eyes and quietly sat down in the corner, occasionally flashing her a nervous look, pleading:

"It's cool. Look. I'm not even looking at you. See?"

I imagined Bramble lying in the corner of the crate, a smug smirk on her face, while the other four dogs shuffled around to give her a quiet 'high four.'

Marley's such a strong dog too, with a low centre of gravity. And he's always in such a rush. Time and tide, and Marley, wait for no man.

"The park. Come on, we're going to the park! The ball. Bring the ball! Come on. Hurry up. Let's go."

And off he'll charge, oblivious to the fact he's still on-lead until we reach the open space.

I may have up to five other dogs in my control, each attached to their leads which will be grasped firmly in my other hand. It wouldn't matter if there were ten, we'll all be dragged along in Marley's wake.

It's been the same since he was a puppy - he's so focussed on getting to the point where the lead comes off, and the tennis ball comes out that nothing else matters. I've read in books that springer spaniels love playing all sorts of games, but particularly ones that involve retrieving a ball. But Marley takes this to a whole different level. In fact, the rules of Marley's game differ from those played by most dogs, in that once retrieved, the ball cannot be given up.

He's a bit on the possessive side, is Marley. Possessive and obsessive.

He seems to think that any ball, or plastic bottle for that matter, within the boundaries of the park where we walk, is his. Or soon will be.

On a few occasions Marley has been known to chase after, and burst, footballs that have been kicked over the fence that separates the designated play-area from the rest of the park.

Awkward.

It's not just balls and drink containers that he believes he's been granted dominion over. One summer's day we walked, just the two of us, through the local woods to the park. Marley was off-lead as usual, and raced ahead.

We entered the park at the point where the local kids were jumping off the rocks into the icy, but calm river. They were naturally blissfully unaware of Marley's impending whirlwind arrival. Had they known he was fast approaching, they surely wouldn't have been so careless as to leave their outer clothing so close to the path.

By the time I breathlessly caught up to Marley, there was something hanging from the corner of his mouth. He sat there, a look of proud, self-satisfaction on his face, while exuding an innocent air of:

'What, me?'

If dogs could whistle, I imagine he'd have been casually doing so while avoiding direct eye contact with me.

I managed to open his jaws and found to my horror that he'd picked up and half eaten some lad's football sock, leaving just three inches of it trailing from the side of his mouth. I started gently pulling. Gradually, like a magician drawing a line of knotted handkerchiefs from a top-hat, I succeeded in retrieving the saliva-soaked sock from the back of Marley's throat.

By now, a crowd of laughing youngsters had gathered round.

"Erm, sorry about that," I sheepishly offered to the sock's owner, handing it to him by my finger-tips.

Exit stage left.

I have become guilty of humanizing the dogs.

It's very easily done when the bulk of the working day is spent in the absence of human contact. I could talk to myself as I walked, but people would think me mad. So I attribute characters to each of the dogs – and talk to them instead. Sometimes I even answer on their behalf.

For instance, Marley represents the loving, hyper-active and independent kid who would sometimes appear rather distant from the rest of class.

Dougal, on the other hand, is the cheeky and naughty show-off that the teacher would invariably sit directly in front of her desk. For 'classroom terror,' read Border terrier.

Like Marley, he's obsessive over balls, sticks, plastic bottles or whatever he can carry in his mouth. However, where Marley tends to hover anti-socially on the edge of the pack, treating the prize as Gollum would his 'precious,' Dougal uses it to tease the others.

"Chase me, chase me. Come and get it."

With his short, compact stature, boundless energy and nimble feet, he's confident of outrunning and out-manoeuvring all-comers. Eventually though, his predictable success backfires when the pack becomes bored with his boastful displays, and he'll drop the object in some quiet spot when nobody else is watching.

An empty beer can which he found discarded in the local woods once provided Dougal with a full half hour of fun. Picking it up with the opened end in his mouth, he bounced around the other dogs, trying to goad them into the chase.

There seemed to be a collective sigh as the pack carried on doing what dogs do when they are released outdoors after several hours cooped up in an empty house.

"Here he goes again." Harry, Buddy, Molly and Murphy looked at each other.

Dougal decided to encourage their participation. Barking excitedly into the empty can, his voice was transformed. There was an echo. That was the signal for interest from the others. For the next thirty minutes, Dougal barked into the can whilst being chased by four dogs each eager for a chance to hear how their voices could be similarly altered.

We've all been to parties where some wise-guy decides to suck the helium from a balloon and then recite Hamlet's 'To be or not to be' soliloquy, right?

Perhaps Dougal's little episode was the doggy equivalent.

Maybe humanizing the animals isn't quite as absurd as it sounds.

*****

6. THE PSYCHOPATHS

Most pets I care for exhibit certain individual eccentricities; harmless little foibles that define their character. There are some however that just have behavioural issues, plain and simple.

Take Muffin for example. Soon after she entered our house, I certainly wished somebody would. Take her away that is.

Muffin was a female house rabbit, who it seems had more freedom in her comfortable terraced house in Glasgow than did the rabbits on the whole expanse of Watership Down. Her owner was going on holiday and couldn't get any family member to look after her while she was away. They were all 'too busy.'

Eight years' experience has taught me now to treat comments like this as a probable warning sign. Back then though, I was naïve, and desperate for business.

I told the owner that Muffin was welcome to stay in one of the secure hutches out in the garage. I have two cats of my own who probably wouldn't be too happy to meet her coming out the kitchen first thing in the morning. House-sharing was not really a great idea.

It was agreed. Muffin returned with me and she was popped into her new temporary home.

Unfortunately, she wouldn't settle. She wouldn't eat. Well, she wouldn't eat food. She was happy to gnaw at, and destroy, the wooden interior of my new hutch, though.

She wasn't happy at all, and the wanton destruction was quite obviously more stress-related than a protest for a more varied diet.

I persevered for a few days. But rather than presenting her owner with a skeletal rabbit upon return from her holiday, I really had no option but to bring Muffin indoors after all.

The door to the office was duly barricaded to prevent the entry of my two naturally curious cats. The metal floor of a large, unused dog-crate was lined with wood shavings. A cat-carry box was filled with straw and placed in the crate to provide a quiet sanctuary for sleeping.

I'd put some thought into this and felt pleased and proud of my effort. Muffin had more room to move around in her new 'des-res' than in her own cage. Granted, she could come and go as she pleased in her normal accommodation, but all things considered, this seemed the perfect, temporary solution.

That night, I was awakened by a frightful banging noise. I quietly slipped out of bed and in hushed voice asked my wife where my baseball bat was. I took it from the back of the wardrobe and sneaked downstairs. As I reached the bottom step, the noise rose again. Three bangs this time.

It was coming from the office. Momentarily forgetting our temporary guest, I feared the worst and wondered whether to lash out first or wait for the intruder to make the initial move. I slowly opened the door and peered into the room.

There were no human shadows. Relief. My tensed body relaxed.

Just then, the light from the hallway behind me met Muffin's eyes, reflecting a piercing glint of red through the darkness. At that moment I realised I was dealing with the Devil's own rabbit – Satan's Little Helper.

Muffin was having a fit; not of a physiological sort, just the 'hissy' type more associated with young children who cannot get their own way. In a show of temper she was thumping her hind legs on the metal floor of the cage to create a dreadful din.

I needed to get back to bed. I gave in.

I allowed her out the cage and onto the carpet, where she promptly laid a neat, but not so little, pile of rabbit poo. She then hopped over to the tasty-looking power cables for my laptop and record-turntable. Before she could become more highly charged than the famous 'Duracell Bunny,' I swept her up and placed her back in the cage.

It was a long night.

Her behaviour became even worse after that. Cleaning her cage became a daily battle of wits – a battle she predictably won because her teeth and claws were infinitely sharper than mine.

A couple of days later, she sank her teeth into my wrist as I tried to remove her food bowl to top it up. I drew my hand away. She drew blood. As I pulled away, she locked her jaws onto my skin and hung on. With her back legs now clear of the ground, her body extended to its full length while my wrist supported her entire weight.

Ignoring the blood now dripping onto the carpet, I managed to open her jaws and release myself from her pseudo death-grip.

The rest of her stay was rather tense to say the least.

I had never been scratched and bitten so much by any animal - but I hadn't at that point met Minstrel, the psychotic cat.

Looks can be so deceptive.

Minstrel was (probably still is, but it's kind of cathartic for me to talk of her in the past tense) a lovely looking long-haired cross-breed female cat. A beautiful blend of black, tan and white.

I knew she'd be a problem from the first time I saw her.

When I met with the owners to discuss details of their requirements, it was very quickly apparent they had placed their first family pet on a pedestal. Or settee.

Mum – I want to sit over there," said one of the family's children, in a whiny intonation.

"Not now, darling," came the sincere reply. "Minstrel's sitting there. Wait till she gets down and you can have the seat."

I got the distinct impression that this type of conversation was not uncommon. Allowing Minstrel to dictate the terms of the pet / owner relationship was surely asking for trouble.

"She's a lovely cat. So good natured," continued the kid's mother. "She's never hurt any of the kids."

Not only alarm bells, but a siren and red flashing lights were raging in my head.

Why would she say such a thing?

I was definitely having doubts about this cat already, but carried on regardless. I noted the security details for entering the house in the owners' absence. I recorded the feeding requirements for their precious pet. I jotted down a couple of other little tasks they wanted me to do.

This was to be the family's first holiday away from their pet, and they took some reassuring that everything would be fine. I'd looked after numerous other cats while their owners were away. Minstrel would be fine. They needn't worry.

My final question to all new clients, is to ask for details of the vet they are registered with – just in case some attention is required in their absence.

"Oh, it's the one in the village, but I think we'll be changing. He doesn't know how to handle Minstrel. He wears this big, heavy leather glove when examining her."

I left with the distinct impression that someone was living in denial.

I figured I knew what to expect when I visited on day one of the clients' holiday.

Minstrel greeted me at the door, instantly rolled over to be tickled, and purred contentedly.

Damn, I was good at this Pet Professional lark. Maybe I'd been a bit too harsh in my initial assessment.

No, I hadn't.

Without any warning she took her first swipe at my hand.

I simply backed off, left her alone. I made my way to the conservatory where one of my additional tasks was to water the indoor plants and open the small windows each morning, closing them again in the evening.

It was summer and I was wearing shorts. This really played right into Minstrel's paws.

I'm not the tallest, and stretching up to open and close fourteen small windows was leaving me a little exposed. I hadn't really considered the possibility of an attack on the blind side though, until I felt Minstrel's sharp claws tearing the flesh from my bare calves.

"She'll settle," I told myself, although they were not the first words I uttered, I have to confess.

Day two was the same as I ran the gauntlet of Minstrel's claws … and she in turn ran them the length of my lower legs.

Day three however brought a new development. Teeth.

Minstrel was peeved I hadn't heeded her earlier warnings, so it was now time for a full-on frontal assault. With a completely unprovoked hiss, Minstrel launched herself at my right shin, sinking her two canine teeth into what limited amount of flesh there is around the human shin-bone.

As the blood ran down my leg (the word 'trickled' is grossly inadequate here) and gathered at the top of my sock, the door-bell rang. It was the rather horrified neighbour who had been asked to water the garden plants in the owners' absence. On seeing my van outside the house, she called round to ensure everything was all right. She was concerned for the cat. Every time she had gone into the garden, Minstrel would make a frenzied charge at the conservatory window and begin meowing loud enough to be heard through the double glazing.

"It's as if she's really stressed," she said, her voice trailing off as she caught a glimpse of my leg. I turned to show her my calves.

"She's probably just a little annoyed that she can't get at your throat," I said in a rather weak attempt at a joke.

Any concern she harboured for Minstrel quickly vanished.

The following morning, I was feeling quite pleased with myself, having pulled on a pair of wellies before entering the house. This is Scotland, remember – it's advisable to carry an 'in case of need' pair with you at all times. And I certainly needed them.

Minstrel watched me attend my duties from a distance, looking a little perplexed by my protection. Similarly, come the evening visit, she was quiet and subdued and I did what I had to do completely unchallenged.

The lesson here though is: never trust a quiet cat.

Come the next visit, I quickly realised the reason she had been so restrained the previous evening. She had been thinking. Scheming. Developing a plan.

Somewhat smugly, I again entered the house flaunting my protected legs, bade Minstrel a chirpy "Good Morning," walked by her and headed towards the conservatory. She instantly broke into a run, overtook me in the doorway to the lounge and jumped atop one of the two settees that were positioned next to each other.

The only way past was via the small gap between them.

I was starting to feel like a cowboy from an old Western movie riding into a canyon knowing that the Indians were watching him from above.

There was no alternative route. I cautiously continued onward, only for Minstrel to let out a blood-curdling growl and launch herself straight at my chest.

What followed was like a scene from a Tom and Jerry cartoon, as her claws sought purchase through my shirt and into my skin. Her grip was only tenuous however, and she gradually began to slowly slide down my front, leaving a few red welts that were going to take some explaining when I got home.

There was nothing else for it: from that day until the owners returned, it was simply a case of throwing a towel over Minstrel as soon as I got into the house, carrying her into another room and locking her in until I was finished my visit.

Normally, I'd leave a note for the returning owners letting them know how their pet had settled. In turn, most owners send a card or text message of thanks.

On this occasion however, I simply wrote on the invoice: 'Hope you had a lovely holiday,' sensing discretion the better part of candour.

A few days later, the clients' cheque was received in the post. There was no expression of gratitude. There was no interest as to how Minstrel had been in their absence.

I think they knew.

*****

7. THE OUTDOORS

Generally speaking, the working day is spent walking in the magnificent, rolling environs of rural Renfrewshire, in the West of Scotland.

Eight years after starting the business, I still find it fascinating to witness at first hand the sights, sounds and smells of the changing seasons: the bright, fresh, clear air of spring, pierced by shrill birdsong; the warm, muggy but perfumed atmosphere of summer permeated by the almost constant hum of the farmers' machinery in the verdant fields. Who wouldn't enjoy the dank, mist-enshrouded, shortening daylight hours of autumn, with the rustle and musty scent of fallen leaves? Even the stark trees and the solid, frozen ground of winter with its icy chill and wind factor that renders the nose incapable of smelling anything at all. It's all wonderful.

Then there's also the added bonus of watching the local wildlife as it goes about its daily business. Normally blinded by our own hectic lifestyles, it's easy to miss just how much is actually going on. The countryside is an amazingly busy place.

The parliament of rooks is in perpetual motion as birds fly in and out of the rookery in the continual search for food or nesting materials. Their seemingly constant, bad-tempered, bickering and the incessant chattering of nearby magpies creates a cacophony that shatters the otherwise tranquil surroundings.

It amuses me to think of the irritated magpies complaining:

"Hey you guys! How about keeping the noise down? We need to concentrate - we're trying to count our haul of shiny things."

Squirrels too, such industrious little animals, rush around hiding and retrieving their food larders. That is, of course, until by chance they attract the attention of a fun-seeking springer spaniel.

Smaller birds: bullfinches, robins, tits and sparrows, flit around the hedgerows, whilst on the ground, rabbits and deer are spotted with frequent regularity. Sometimes, a faint movement within the undergrowth will alert me to a fleeing mouse, shrew or occasionally a rat.

It's all very interesting, but for me there's nothing much more exciting than being startled by an even more startled brown hare. First its ears prick up to their full extent then, in a flash, it takes off, covering the ground at speeds and for distances that no domestic pet could possibly compete.

I remember a hare being chased across a field by two galloping horses, who in turn were being vainly pursued by a dog from the local farm. It was like a scene from a Benny Hill TV sketch – all that was missing was the iconic music.

I heartily recommend taking time out to explore Nature's exciting sights, both above our heads and below our feet. There's so much goes unnoticed.

However, it may also be possible to stumble across some wonderful and unexpected spectacles completely by chance.

For instance, although I've lived in this area for twenty-five years, I was not aware of the nesting kingfisher birds down by the river. Not, until the day Buddy, the cute and fluffy, but over-confident and excitable Japanese spitz dog had to be unceremoniously fished out of it.

More obvious in their presence are the herons who, provided the dogs are kept at a safe distance, are happy to continue with their patient stalking and fishing whilst being watched.

And if it's 'cute,' you want, then what better than to watch a mother duck guide her brood of ducklings through the water to the sanctuary of a calm pool, sheltered by the trailing branch of a riverbank tree.

The local ducks make me smile. Especially after heavy rainstorms, of which we get many, when they use the swollen and fast-moving river like a thrilling ride in a theme park.

They fly about a hundred and fifty metres upriver to where it is relatively calm, and settle on the surface. From there, they paddle like fury until they reach the newly created, nearby rapids, letting the rushing water carry them, bobbing up and down, to where it calms again.

However, it's not all fun, sweetness and light where Mother Nature is concerned – she also has a dark side and wicked sense of humour, as I would discover.

*****

8. THE DANGERS

Belle, a small brown and white springer spaniel, was only booked to walk with me for a week while her owner recuperated from a bout of ill health. So perhaps she felt there was no need to learn a new set of commands.

"I know these fields like the back of my paw – I walk up here every day with my proper master. I don't need direction; I know what I'm doing. This new guy needn't worry, I'll head back to him just as soon as I've checked out this wild and interesting scent. What's he so worried about? Chill, my friend. Chill. What could possibly go wrong?"

Belle raced up the hill to our right, a long, drag of a hill, extending some three hundred metres away from the loch at the bottom. It was late morning on a hot July day, but surprisingly, the local beauty spot was devoid of any other human life for as far as the eye could see.

My shouts for Belle to return fell on deaf ears and with the distance between us growing by the minute, it was apparent she was on a mission.

There was now no alternative. I gave in and began a rather undignified chase up the hill. A couple of minutes later and perspiring profusely, I was with her. But our troubles were just about to begin.

Springers are notoriously focused dogs, and Belle was so frantic in her search for the source of the scent that she hadn't noticed, or even heard, the commotion that was now developing some ten metres above her head.

It suddenly dawned on me; we must have strayed into the territory of a pair of nesting buzzards. These not-so- little raptors are fiercely territorial, and with it being highly likely there were fledglings sitting in the nest, this adult was going to make sure we wandered no closer.

It targeted me first, swooping down to perhaps only two metres above my head. It made a few passes, screeching its threats and doing its level best to scare me away. A mew-like call came from the trees. The buzzard's mate was still in the nest, and letting it be known that Belle had strayed closer and presented more of a danger. The attacker swiftly diverted its attention to the completely oblivious dog.

She wasn't oblivious for long.

Perhaps feeling emboldened by Belle's smaller stature, the bird plummeted to within two feet of her head. It took a couple of dives, but Belle eventually got the message. She firstly looked up in utter astonishment, and then glanced in my direction as if to ask what I was going to do about all this.

"I thought you were meant to be looking after me?"

She'd suddenly changed her tune. She wasn't so cocky now.

"This way Belle," I suggested. "Run."

I whistled once and Belle was by my side, escorted from about three metres above by a victorious and no doubt gloating, buzzard. We raced back down the hill to the van, presumably all the time under the watchful eye of our determined aggressor.

We didn't look back to check.

A valuable lesson was learnt that day: a bird of prey hovering above your head is not hanging around to hear your excuses or apologies.

I was with three dogs, all from the same household: Ozzie, a bouncy, athletic and energetic bearded collie cross; Gem, a lovely-natured little Staffordshire bull terrier; and Sam, a rather overweight, but ultra-sociable Cairn terrier whose short, stumpy legs struggle to keep his belly from trailing the ground.

In a country park, high in the hills that overlook Paisley and Glasgow, we were following our regular route. As normal, I checked each field for sheep and cattle before entering. Except, on this occasion the cattle were not apparent from the entrance and were actually ensconced in an obscured dip, around a bend.

The three dogs were off-lead and slightly ahead of me as they charged through the open ground. Well, Ozzie and Gem, at least – Sam was mooching his way around as usual, searching for scraps of discarded picnic food and leaving his scent-mark on just about every raised tuft of grass that he passed.

I knew something was wrong the instant all three stopped what they were doing and stood still. Gem threw me a look from over her shoulder which I loosely translated as:

"We've got a problem …"

Confronting us now, and quickly rising to their feet, were about twenty cows. Worse - they each had their young with them.

I returned Gem's look, hoping she'd interpret it as:

"Keep calm, and walk slowly towards the woods."

At least in there, I reckoned, the cattle would have no room to charge us, and if we were seen to be walking away from them, hopefully they'd realise we intended no harm to their calves.

The most vociferous of the herd was by now no more than four metres from me. She was snorting and stamping her front hooves on the ground. The others were becoming more animated and vocal as they circled us. I shot a look towards the wooded area, some fifty metres away.

The alarmed baying of the group in front of us had alerted a splinter-herd, who had been resting-up in the shade of the very same woods.

Gem slowly turned her head towards me, a quizzical look on her face. I think she was saying:

"What now, wise-guy?"

'What now?' indeed.

Well, Ozzie, being of nimble foot, had already made himself scarce and scarpered towards the bottom end of the field. Gem, ever so trusting, was still awaiting instruction.

Sam, completely unaware of any possible danger, decided he'd like to make friends with the cattle. This was not helping, at all.

A car stopped on the road that bisects the park, and the driver came to the fence around a hundred metres away. From his vantage point, down the slope from where we were cornered, he could see a gap forming in the herd. He shouted to me and pointed to where we should run.

And run we did – Gem close by my side.

It was, as I'd read in magazine articles, 'every man and dog for themselves,' as we, the faithful Gem and myself, raced through the break in formation. Sam, however was still dithering around with his new 'pals.'

"Come on Sam" I hollered. "BISCUITS!"

That did the trick. His little legs were a blur as he tried to catch up, more afraid of missing out on a treat than the danger of being trampled and kicked to death by an irate cow or two.

We quickly reached the sanctuary of the road, where Ozzie was waiting:

"What kept you?" I could imagine him panting.

*****

9. THE ADRENALINE

What surprised me about the episodes with the buzzard and cattle, was the fact that I managed to remain reasonably calm, despite the adrenaline coursing through my body.

There were many moments in my time as a Bank Manager that I could liken that to, but one in particular still quickens my heart-rate when I recall it: the second armed raid on my Branch in a fortnight!

Whereas the first was a rather quiet, subdued, one-man-job, the other was by an organised gang – balaclavas, similar coloured clothing, hand-gun, and machete. With his gun pointed directly at my face from only a few metres away, the gang-leader yelled at me to bring him the safe keys.

I could see all my staff lying face-down on the floor, some screaming in terror. Yet despite part of my brain going into meltdown, the other half was calmly counting the time the raiders had been in the office. Knowing that they wouldn't want to stick around more than thirty seconds or so, I delayed doing as he demanded. Thankfully, just as the still functioning part of my brain reasoned, the raiders made off only with what they could grab from the counter.

There is good reason for relating this anecdote.

Early one Sunday morning, I was walking Hugo and Humphrey, two miniature schnauzers, along a rough track that runs through the woods of a neighbouring village. Normally popular with locals out for a stroll, this was well before the church bells rang out calling them to worship, so it appeared we had the area to ourselves.

But we didn't.

Ten minutes into the walk, a car slowly approached from the far end of the woods. It didn't look much like a farm vehicle, which was the only type to use the track in my experience. I called the dogs back by my side. As the car passed, I could see the four occupants stare intently at me. They were big lads, and whatever their business was, it looked like they meant it.

It all appeared a bit suspicious – why were four reasonably young men in a car, on a lonely woodland track, at this early hour, and on a Sunday? Strange.

But we had a walk to complete, so we carried on.

A few minutes later, another car appeared, this time with a bit more urgency. It drew up alongside us, the occupants keen to talk. They were five policemen in an unmarked vehicle. Not only were they fully uniformed, but they wore flak jackets and carried what looked like sub-machine guns!

Had I seen anything or anyone suspicious in the woods?

"Yeah – a few minutes ago a car passed with four shady looking guys in it," I offered.

"Apart from them – they're plain clothes officers," came the terse reply.

"Oops, sorry. No – I'm afraid not. Why?" I asked.

"Because there's just been an armed raid on the village store and the culprit was last seen heading into these woods about ten minutes ago. I'd get yourself out of here as fast as you can if I were you," came the more friendly advice.

What's the saying? 'Been there; seen it; done it; got the T-shirt.' I didn't need to be advised twice.

Perhaps not quite so dramatic, but inducing an adrenaline rush all the same, was an on-lead walk with a very, very timid miniature poodle called Dulcie, and her tiny housemate, Lulu, a spunky but elderly and partially blind bichon frise.

We had strayed along a single track country lane and were about two hundred metres from a farmhouse. In the distance, I could hear some aggressive barking and the frantic recall shouts of a woman.

Through my binoculars, I saw that the noisy farm dogs had stopped for a moment. They glanced at each other, and then back at the woman. It looked very much like they were having a meeting to discuss whether they should obey the command or not.

The vote favoured the 'not,' option.

Two of the four dogs were large dobermans. That was all I needed. I didn't really care about the others now. They were headed our way. And in a hurry.

I was truly impressed at just how quickly a doberman can cover a hundred metres. But with the initial distance between us already halved, it was time for action.

We couldn't make a run for it – Dulcie was already frozen to the spot. The only movement she was likely to make would have been a rather smelly one. Picking them both up wasn't an option either, as the aggressors would only jump upon me to get to them

Rather than my life flashing before my eyes, I was conscious of a fleeting thought: how could I explain to the owners that their dear pets were a bloodied mess and perhaps missing a leg or two?

Then came that 'eureka' moment.

Back in the Eighties, Barbara Woodhouse became a household name for her dog-training methods. I remembered her writing that a dog responds best to, 'tone of voice, telepathy and a little bit of loving.'

There wasn't time to incorporate all three components, and I wasn't exactly in a mood for any 'loving,' at that precise moment. I instinctively dropped that one in favour of the other two.

I prayed telepathy mirrored wishful thinking, and with the advancing dogs now less than twenty metres away, I placed both Dulcie and Lulu's leads in my right hand. I held out my left, palm facing the sky, and pulling it directly to my shoulder, I said loudly, and in my best, shrill and very 'proper' Barbara Woodhouse voice:

"SIT!"

One word … that's all it took. The dobermans and their pals came to an immediate halt. They didn't sit down, but instead gave each other a startled, quizzical and almost incredulous look, turned away and quickly walked back to the farm.

She certainly knew her stuff, did dear old Barbara.

I looked down – poor Dulcie was quivering uncontrollably with fright.

Lulu either hadn't seen the whole incident – or was in a self-congratulatory mood, skipping back down the road in the belief that her naturally courageous demeanour had repelled the would-be attackers.

*****

10. THE ACCIDENTS

Accidents happen in all walks of life. Dog walks included.

Even with a vigilant eye, keen anticipation and an acute awareness of potential hazards, these incidents are inevitable when walking up to six dogs at a time. There's the almost daily problem of unhitching dogs caught by their collar on a farmer's wire fence; dragging oversized dogs from undersized ditches - and worse, undersized dogs from oversized ditches. But thankfully, in my eight years as a Pet Professional, I have had to cope with only two serious ones.

Marley the springer spaniel was at the centre of the most worrying.

It was a hot summer's day and the lunch-time pack of six had almost reached the half-way point in our walk. They had just been for a swim to cool off, and now refreshed, were chasing each other around the bushes on the riverbank.

By now, they had given up all hope of getting the tennis ball from Marley, who in turn was comforted by the fact that the others made no further attempts to steal it. He now dropped it at my feet, his tail whirling in a circular motion, tongue lolling in anticipation of the chase.

I kicked the ball a short distance, only twenty metres or so, and it landed in a clump of overgrown grass and weed just off the main path. Marley raced after it, confident he knew where it had settled. His leap looked almost feline, his big ears extending to the sides like two furry wings as he pounced.

There was a loud, sharp shriek. Then nothing. Silence.

Marley stood absolutely still.

But Marley doesn't 'do' standing still. Something was seriously wrong.

I saw immediately his eyes were glazed. He stared at me, but it was a vacant stare. I checked his paws for any embedded thorns or shards of glass. Nothing. There was no blood evident anywhere on his body and there were no obvious breaks or strains to his legs. He tentatively turned in the direction of the van, which was still a good half mile away. He definitely wanted me to get him home, quickly. This was not like Marley at all.

He stood, mouth agape. Perhaps he'd swallowed a bee or a wasp, and been stung in the throat? I checked for any swelling in his mouth but found nothing untoward.

By now, Marley was quite emphatic in his attempts to return to the van so I hooked him back onto his lead. Two of the remaining dogs, black labradors, continued to play, oblivious to the drama that had quietly unfolded just a few metres away. The other three, however, had sensed something was not right and were already by my side, ready for their leads to be attached.

I called the final two over. They saw what was happening and where I would normally expect some resistance to stopping play, they immediately trotted across.

It was a very quiet and well behaved walk back to the van, the pack perhaps concerned as to Marley's predicament.

The priority now was to deliver Marley back to his home as quickly as possible. His owner's mother was alone in the house. I offered to take Marley directly to the local vet, but it was left that she'd phone her daughter for a decision on what to do.

I suggested Marley be left to lie quietly and that I'd call back in an hour or so to see how he was. Thankfully, when I did, his owners had returned early from work and were preparing to take him to the vet.

A couple of hours later, they appeared at my house with a traumatised and heavily sedated Marley in the back of their car. They presented me with a sealed, clear plastic envelope, inside which was a twig, some three inches long. This had been the cause of Marley's distress. It had pierced the lining and passed through the wall of his pharynx, finally resting alongside the oesophagus area.

Nasty.

It now made perfect sense - when he frantically leapt for the ball, Marley didn't see the upright stick hidden amongst the tangle of long grass and weeds. On landing, his open mouth connected first with the twig which plunged deep into the recess of his throat.

Poor soul. He cut such a forlorn image that evening.

Nothing keeps Marley down for long though, and after a couple of quiet days' rest, he was back out with the pack, fearlessly chasing down that little yellow tennis ball.

Japanese spitz dogs are little whirlwinds of brilliant white fur. Standing only about two feet tall, their luxuriant coat exaggerates their body size, yet despite this they are plucky wee things, afraid of nothing.

So when Buddy's lead pulled taut and remained so, even after a gentle tug, I knew something was wrong.

"Come on Buddy," I cajoled. "Time to go. Straight back to house, now."

We had finished our lunchtime walk, and with all five dogs now tethered to their leads, were heading along the leafy lane that ran adjacent to the field in which we'd just walked.

Buddy was resolute. He wasn't for moving. I pulled again. Buddy looked at me pleadingly. Puzzled at his reaction, I glanced at his hind quarters and saw what I thought was a large twig tangled up in his coat.

On closer inspection, however, I realised that a length of rusted barbed wire had wrapped itself around his back-right leg. It extended up into his midriff and, I feared, his genital area. No wonder he yelped and bit me as I tried to release him from the vicious barbs.

After a few more failed attempts that elicited several more successful bites, it became clear I would not be able to free Buddy from the painful grasp of the wire.

He quickly learnt that his best option was to remain stationary. The other four dogs, to their credit, were not presenting too much of a problem. I'm sure they sensed their pal's predicament.

They couldn't have realised mine.

We were about a hundred metres from the main road that runs through the village, and obscured from view by an area of overgrown woodland. There was no way of attracting the attention of anyone passing by.

Keep calm, I told myself. What would Timmy Martin do in this situation?

Actually, the more I thought about it, Timmy wouldn't have had to deal with this at all as Lassie would have noticed the offending stretch of barbed wire and barked out a warning to the other dogs. But this thought process wasn't helping.

I phoned another dog-walker I knew in the village.

"Suzanne – are you anywhere near Houston right now? We have a problem."

Fortunately, Suzanne was only five minutes away.

"Ouch! That looks painful. Poor Buddy – do you want me to go get some wire clippers from my house? We could snip the wire at a manageable length to at least free him, and then you could take him to the vet." Suzanne lived only a couple minutes' walk away. She also knew wee Buddy as she'd covered for me while I was on holiday a few months earlier.

"Thanks, but no," I decided. "I don't want to risk any harm, and anyway, I'd still have to carry Buddy back to my car and then to the vet. If you put the other dogs back in my car – it's just down the road at Buddy's house – then I'll be able to keep Buddy calm and call the S.S.P.C.A. for advice and help."

The S.S.P.C.A. is the Scottish equivalent of the English Royal Society for the Prevention of Cruelty to Animals.

I made the call and spent the next forty minutes waiting with a rather distressed, but at least calm, Buddy. It began to rain. We both felt miserable. Granted, Buddy considerably more so than me.

The two S.S.P.C.A. officers that duly arrived were tremendous. After a few minutes gaining his trust, a bandage was used to muzzle Buddy and he was gently turned onto his side. I firmly held his head steady while one of the officers gripped his back legs and unceremoniously prised them apart to reveal the extent of the wire's intrusion.

And, yes, it was lying perilously close to his 'bits.'

The second officer then proceeded to delicately cut Buddy's fur away from the wire. Ten minutes later, and following a further examination, Buddy was free. With bald patches.

My concern was that he would never trust me again for putting him through such an ordeal. I needn't have worried. With the first mention of the word 'biscuit,' the events of the past hour or so seemed long forgotten.

There isn't much a Pet Professional can realistically do to avoid some accidents.

But, the hamster incident? With the benefit of hindsight, this one could have been averted.

Two related families in the village were going on holiday together. The young daughters, cousins, each had a hamster and boarded them with me while they were away. Both hamsters were of the Syrian variety, male and the same age, about one and a half years.

One, Biscuit, enjoyed a simple lifestyle. He was housed in a basic cage with little in the way of additional toys, was fed just regular hamster food and received no edible treats. He was friendly, obviously used to being handled, and the owner seemed happy enough to pass him over to me.

The other, Toffee, luxuriated in more materialistic surroundings. He had it all: a cage about twice the size of Biscuit's; several different toys and plastic tunnels to play in; superior quality hamster food and a variety of goodies such as flavoured yoghurt-dipped snacks and fruity seed-sticks. His owner kissed him goodbye with tear filled eyes.

Syrian hamsters are notoriously independent little rodents and as adults are very quarrelsome in company. With that in mind, I placed their cages several feet apart, on top of a five-foot high shelving unit.

Looking at their comparative living conditions, it was hard not to feel a little sorry for Biscuit.

But Biscuit was not one to wallow in self-pity.

It was mid-afternoon on the second day of their stay and having topped up Biscuit's food, I closed his cage door. Just as I released the catch to Toffee's swanky home, the shrill tone of my house phone interrupted me. I closed the cage door over and left the room to take the call.

Ten minutes later, while upstairs doing something completely unrelated I heard a loud hissing and squawking noise that lasted about thirty seconds.

I gave it no more than a passing thought. It could be one of two things: either my two cats were squabbling, or maybe the magpies and rooks were chasing the squirrels away from the garden bird-table.

Actually, it was one of three things. And it was the third.

Forty-five minutes later, I remembered I still hadn't topped up Toffee's food.

I returned to my office, where the hamsters were boarding. I was horrified to see traces of blood running along the front side of Toffee's cage.

"Perhaps he's stressed by his new surroundings and been too enthusiastic in chewing the metal bars," I thought. I peeked into his bedding area to see if he'd settled.

To my dismay, Toffee was covered in blood and trembling uncontrollably.

Once I had cleaned him up, I could see he had what appeared to be a small bite mark on the back of his neck. I then noticed that his honey-stick treat was no longer hanging from his cage. Well, the stick part was still there, but it was stripped bare. There were a couple of small pieces lying on the floor of his cage.

The penny dropped as to what the earlier noise had been, and I looked into Biscuit's cage. Curled up in his bedding and snoozing contentedly, he looked the epitome of innocence.

However, incriminating, broken chunks of honey-stick, strewn throughout his cage revealed a more sinister character.

It's rather pointless trying to reprimand a hamster, so I didn't bother. And although I later discovered the door to Biscuit's basic cage was faulty, and wouldn't snap shut fully, I had to concede my part in the incident. Before taking the phone call, I should have made absolutely certain that the doors to both cages were properly closed.

Fortunately, my local vet is also a friend and he agreed to see little Toffee straight away. There was no lasting damage and a simple, seven-day course of antibiotics was prescribed.

All good - except Toffee was due to be returned to his doting owner in five days.

Now came the tricky bit.

Although absolutely fine, save a little scab that had formed on the back of his neck, I felt I had to be up front with the customers. I assured them that Toffee had received the best of veterinary attention. However, should there be any repercussions with his health, then the vet had been instructed to invoice me for any further treatment.

The little girl was naturally a bit upset. Her father was pretty angry. Thankfully though, neither asked if it was their cousin's pet that had mugged poor Toffee.

I haven't heard from them since – my only unhappy clients.

*****

11. THE FEAR

Certain dog breeds are guaranteed to instil wariness in the minds of those they come across; an apprehension that can quickly descend into fear. Sometimes this may be a justified reaction, although more often not.

In the case of Brose and Dragan it was justified.

Both dogs came from the same household.

Brose was a large, excitable and bouncy dalmation who always seemed to be wearing a smile.

Dragan was a cross between a Staffordshire bull terrier and some indistinguishable brute of a dog in Poland, from where he'd arrived with his owner when she moved to the UK. He was devilishly strong, over twice the size of a standard staffie, but with a similarly low centre of gravity.

I first met them when chatting with Gaye, their original walker. She controlled them on short chain-leads in addition to having secondary leads attached to her belt. I initially thought this a little strange, but it turns out this was for good reason.

When she decided to streamline her business, Gaye offered Brose and Dragan to various other dog-walkers in the area.

Several tried. All failed. Not so much because the dogs would misbehave, although they did have their mischievous moments, but because of their strength. Dragan in particular. Whether he wanted to turn left or right, there was really not much point arguing.

Now at the desperation stage, the owners approached me.

I was blissfully unaware of the trouble they'd encountered having Brose and Dragan walked and although ostensibly fully booked, the promise of five bookings per week for fifty weeks of the year prompted me to reassess my diary.

On a cold and icy Scottish winter's morning, I met with my new clients at their home.

I had rather lazily and incorrectly convinced myself that the name 'Dragan,' referred in some way to Satan. So, on entering the house and being shown through to the living room I was more than a little surprised, and in truth initially horrified, to see this bruiser of a dog snuggling up to the owners' eighteen months old twin girls. Even if he was supervised.

Brose on the other hand, totally ignored the toddlers, being way too excited about my presence. He immediately stood up on his hind legs, and placed his front paws on my shoulders. With his tail whipping against the legs of the dining table, he began to lick the recently applied moisturiser off my face.

I had a new best friend.

Two days later, I took the two dogs for their first walk.

The owners requested I keep Dragan on-lead throughout the walk, but Brose could wander off-lead if I felt comfortable to let him do so.

"Normal-sized sticks don't really hold an interest for Dragan. So if he does somehow slip your grasp, then look for a small log. He loves to carry or chew on them, and he'll usually abandon whatever had prompted his escape, to come collect it from you."

Logs. Not sticks. This perhaps best illustrates the size and strength of Dragan.

It was mid-afternoon and we headed to where their owners walked them at weekends. It's a community woodland area, popular with dog owners, bird-watchers and ramblers. On any given day, you're likely to come across kestrels, great spotted woodpeckers, buzzards and hen harriers. And sheep.

Brose likes sheep. I now know this. Or maybe he dislikes them and that's why he'd rip their throats out if he managed to get close enough.

As his stamina seemed impaired by his muscle mass, I virtually had to drag Dragan back to the car park towards the end of our walk. Brose, who had behaved impeccably throughout the walk was still off-lead. He'd walk a little ahead of me, turning occasionally to check my whereabouts.

Suddenly, Brose showed a cheetah-like explosion of pace as a stray ram wandered onto our path some hundred metres away.

My desperate shouts, ignored by the fixated Brose, alerted the ram. It bolted towards the relative sanctuary of some bushes and managed to conceal itself sufficiently until I had caught up with the obsessed dalmation.

Brose ran around the bushes a couple of times, stopping occasionally to listen for any movement. Fortunately, he has the attention span of a hyper-active fruit fly. When he heard me call the word 'biscuits,' his focus altered and he returned to my side.

This guaranteed reward was infinitely more appealing than the possibility of mutton without carrots, potatoes and currant sauce.

It was, by now, gone four o'clock. Parents, having collected their children from school, were looking forward to a relaxing walk with their kids and dogs through the generally tranquil setting. With two hundred metres remaining to the car park, we met the first of those dog owners. And their pet.

Brose, still off-lead, was first to spot the black labrador, and before I could hook him up, he was gone. Gone in six seconds; off on a confrontational collision course some eighty metres further up the frost-hardened dirt track.

He didn't stand on ceremony and launched straight into the unsuspecting black lab.

Dragan, bless him, also wanted a piece of the action, but it was like comparing Usain Bolt and a Bulgarian shot-putter coming out of their starting blocks. And because he was double-hooked to his leads, Dragan had the added handicap of having to tow me in his wake.

Nevertheless, we managed to reach the point of conflict before too much damage was done.

It certainly wasn't easy, restraining Dragan while trying to part the two feuding dogs and I did suffer some personal collateral damage. However, I managed to separate Brose and pull him away by his collar.

The black lab's owner was very understanding, and having noticed I had inadvertently suffered more bites than her pet, adopted the 'dogs will be dogs,' attitude and carried on her way.

That day I learned exactly why their previous handler kept Brose and Dragan each on two leads.

I learnt also, later that evening, that 'dragan' is actually a masculine Slavic word derived from 'dorgu,' which means 'dear,' in English. I would learn over the course of the next two years walking with him, that Dragan was actually a very apt name. Towards humans, and especially the toddlers in his family, he was so gentle and endearing.

The same could also be said of his housemate, Brose. When alone with me, they were two of the loveliest, good natured dogs I had the pleasure of walking with. Unfortunately, when in the company of their own species, they morphed into a formidable and quite psychopathic combination.

As a result, I changed the time of their walks in the hope that the woods would be quieter at eight in the morning than they were at four in the afternoon.

Initially, we did meet a few others out walking their dogs, but 'once bitten' and all that, I had both my charges doubled-up on the lead front.

And although they viciously strained to reach the poor, terrified innocents, any further fights were thankfully, albeit narrowly, avoided.

As the weeks passed, it became noticeable we were no longer meeting other dogs and owners on the trail. I didn't give it too much thought until the day we were late in starting our walk and as a consequence, about fifteen minutes later than usual in returning to the van.

I was puzzled to see, as we approached the car park, each of the five other cars had people sitting in the driver's seat. Barking could be heard from the back of the cars.

As I loaded my two into the dog crate in the back of the van, I became aware of five other car doors opening, the owners moving to the rear of their vehicle. Suddenly, the car park was filled with a boisterous pack of excited dogs, eager for their early morning walk.

Reputations, it seems, build fast in these parts.

*****

12. THE ESCAPEE

I have a confession to make: I rather enjoy receiving text messages from other dog-walkers, asking me to be on the look-out for one of their lost dogs. It fills me with a warm sense of smugness as I walk with my pack intact.

Does this make me a bad person?

After that initial wave of conceitedness has washed over, however, I have every sympathy for my fellow professionals. For I know the forces of karma await just around the corner. 'There but for the grace of God, go I,' and all that.

Actually, it did happen to me once. But as I knew where the little rascal would be, I prefer not to count it as a strike against me.

Toby was a lovely, bouncy little black and white flecked cocker spaniel. He was only one and a half years old and unconditionally devoted to Morgan, the owner's teenage daughter. She walked him, fussed over and cared for him until the day she moved out of the family home to go live with her boyfriend.

Toby's behaviour changed noticeably in the week following the daughter's departure. He became withdrawn from the rest of the pack. He would trudge rather than skip on the walks, and it was sad to see just how much he missed his teenaged friend.

One week later though, and his spirits were raised. The love of his life had returned and spent the weekend at the family home. When I collected him at lunch-time on the Monday, he was back to his normal, extrovert self.

What he didn't understand though, was that Morgan had only returned for a few days, to collect and move more of her belongings to her new house.

"Bye, Toby – be a good boy. Enjoy your walk."

Those fondly uttered words were the last Toby would hear from the girl for a good while – although he was of course blissfully unaware of this.

Throughout the walk, Toby enthusiastically chased after the teasing crows and jackdaws that dared to land anywhere in his vicinity. He rooted around in the undergrowth, trying hard to sniff out whatever cocker spaniels think is worth the effort. He tried, and failed, to steal the pack's tennis ball from Marley, the large springer.

All was right with his world.

Until we returned to his house, turned the key in the door and entered.

Instantly, I could tell he was on edge. He raced into the hallway. Barking an octave higher than normal, he quickly picked up the scent he was so anxious for; he ran from room to room, his tail slapping like a damp flag in a changeable wind

"Come on Toby, time for bed."

I gently shepherded him into the kitchen with the words reserved to signify the end of that day's walk.

He flashed me an accusing look:

"This is your fault, you know," he seemed to be saying. "Where is she? Why is Morgan not here?"

Poor Toby. He was panicking. He wouldn't settle in his bed; he wouldn't even accept his favourite doggie-treat. There was nothing I could do to placate him, so reluctantly, I left him alone and messaged

Morgan's mother who said she'd leave work early that day to comfort him.

The following day, I was greeted by a very suspicious looking little cocker spaniel. Toby glared at me from his bed as I approached with his lead. In cartoon terms, there was a dark cloud of resentment hovering just above his head.

His lead attached, Toby required a degree of persuasion to follow me to the van. Normally, he'd jump up and greet the pack but today he simply wasn't interested and had to be lifted into the dog-crate.

Arriving at our destination a few minutes later, all six dogs, including Toby, piled out onto the grass, eagerly running in circles, chasing each other and periodically stopping to make their mark.

Toby, however, seemed more interested in fixing his bearings as he plodded around, sniffing the air and determinedly holding back from joining the rest of the group. He did tag on to the tail-end of the pack as we started walking along the riverside. After five minutes, I became conscious of him starting to fall behind; after ten, he was still hanging on there, but my cheeks were becoming sore from persistently whistling him to keep up.

I rounded a bend in the park with the others, heading away from the river. I waited a few moments for Toby. I whistled again. I shouted. Nothing.

I retraced my steps back around the bend, but there was still no sign of Toby. With a dreadful sense of foreboding, I ran to the river.

"Oh, thank you, God," I thought, considering the absence of a floundering dog infinitely more positive than the simple absence of a dog.

Hurriedly, the other dogs were herded together and put back on lead. We immediately started back towards the car, the five remaining dogs no doubt puzzled by the speed of the walk and my constant calling of Toby's name.

My naivety, and controlled panic were evident when stopping the first two dog-owners I met, asking if they had seen a small black and white flecked cocker spaniel. It soon dawned on me this tactic would not augur well for either attracting new business or enhancing my, so far, unblemished reputation.

I decided to take a punt. I loaded the pack back into the van and drove straight to Toby's house in the village, a mile away. And there he was, sitting outside the front door. I wouldn't use the phrase 'without a care in the world,' and neither would I say he was pleased to see me – but at least he was safe.

On each of the following three days when I called to collect Toby, he would remain in his basket, adamant he wasn't leaving the house. If I tried to approach him, he'd spring towards me, attempting to bite.

It was obvious he still associated me with Morgan's leaving. He didn't trust me anymore.

I never walked Toby again.

*****

13. THE DEATHS

As a youngster, I owned several pets: a budgie; a couple of dogs, and several mice. Shortly after being married, my wife and I adopted a kitten, and when our two boys were young, they cared for several gerbils. And a stick insect called Twiggy.

They all died. Of course they did. That's the way it goes.

Some lasted longer than others. Kizzy, the kitten grew graciously into her old age and passed away at the grand old age of eighteen.

Twiggy had an above-average lifespan of around sixteen months. He even survived a day and night on the walk having escaped from his terrarium. Stick insects are not known for their ability to run.

The following morning, we discovered Twiggy sitting on top of a school-bag. Our younger son was convinced that he'd settled there, banking on being spotted and returned to his home, and food supply, when the boys got ready for school.

I digress. The point is – when I decided to work with animals, at some point I knew I'd have to deal with their deaths. In my first eight years as a Pet Professional, there were several. Fortunately, from a purely selfish point of view, these all occurred through natural causes and whilst in the pet-owners' care.

Of course, that's upsetting enough and especially so with dogs where invariably bonds and friendships have been forged, but I dreaded the first pet to die on my watch. It had to happen.

Coco was a large brown adult rabbit, one of three from the same litter who had been boarding with me off and on for a couple of years. I always ask the owners about their pets' health when they bring them to me, but on this occasion I was not around and so the lady simply popped the three rabbits into the hutch.

After a couple of days, I noticed Coco's behaviour change ever so slightly. He was becoming a little withdrawn and by the evening feed, his lethargy was plain to see. The following morning, his breathing had become erratic and his body temperature had dropped.

Telephone calls to his owner went unanswered, so I took the decision to refer Coco to the local vet. After briefly outlining the background and the nature of my concern, the vet began his examination.

Normally, I would have expected to witness some resistance to the probing and prodding, but Coco remained listless and limp. As he made various checks, the vet said:

"He's quite old, isn't he? I think this is just an age-related issue."

He turned Coco around on the rubber-topped and disinfected examination table.

"He's probably not got long to go, you know. It may be as well to just put him to sleep now, and release him from his discomfort."

That really wasn't what I wanted to hear. I was hoping for more of an "I'll give him this little vitamin injection, and he'll be fine by tomorrow morning," type of reply.

I began to mull over the quandary. But before the second "Hmmm, err ..." could be uttered, the decision was taken out my hands.

"Actually, it looks like he's gone already," said the vet, holding the lifeless body of the rabbit in his arms. "He was very weak. Do you want me to keep his body in the refrigerated unit until you contact the owner for disposal instructions?"

I prayed I'd somehow be able to show a little more compassion when explaining everything to my client.

I sent a text to the owner, asking that she contact me as soon as she had time. The rest of that morning I spent rehearsing in my head how I would break the sad news whilst explaining that I did all that was possible for Coco. This was not going to be easy.

"Oh – I wondered how long he'd last," came the surprisingly chirpy response when contact was eventually made later in the day. "He'd not been well for a couple of weeks. Sorry – I forgot to tell you," was the back-up line. "He was a fair age. And, nah, just ask the vet to dispose of the body as normal. I don't need it back."

I was certainly relieved that she seemed to have taken the news so well. But I was also a touch annoyed, on behalf of poor, departed Coco that she took it quite so casually. And yes, I was slightly angered myself that I'd been stressing out over his death for no apparent reason

I wasn't going to dwell on the matter, though. Especially in light of her parting sentence:

"I doubt the other two will last very long either," she mentioned rather glibly.

There were three days to go until she returned from holiday.

I crossed my fingers and counted the minutes.

The death of a beloved pet is always traumatic for the owner. Even more so when the passing is at a pre-determined time, and an upsetting, final journey together is made to the vet's surgery.

I have only had to make that dreaded trip once in a personal capacity, when our eighteen year old cat, Kizzy, had to be put to sleep. Even though I returned to work in the bank in the afternoon, I was a complete mess.

I suppose at least it let my customers see that bank Branch Managers are human after all.

In a professional capacity, I have, to a degree, learnt to distance myself emotionally from the death of a pet I've cared for. Life goes on. I have to earn a living.

There was one particular instance, however, that really tested me.

I'd walked Oscar, a twelve year-old black, flat-coated retriever, three times a week for six years. He was the elder statesman of the pack, occasionally joining in with the chases and play-fights, but generally he stood back and let the young ones get on with it. He was a very undemanding, obedient and sociable dog. One who made my job easy.

Not long after his twelfth birthday, Oscar developed a growth on his head. The vet told his owners that it was inoperable, but shouldn't affect his daily life for a month or two. So, we continued our walks, and indeed Oscar seemed content enough.

But then, a turn for the worse, as the growth suddenly accelerated its development, and within a few more weeks, it had all but closed over one of his eyes. His head became markedly deformed and although he was still happy to walk with the pack, it was coming to the time all owners dread.

He wasn't in any distress at that particular time, but his condition was deteriorating very quickly. Rather than condemn Oscar to any unnecessary suffering, his owners agreed the unenviable but inevitable decision had to be made.

Because he so much enjoyed his lunchtime outings with the pack, the date and time were arranged specifically to fit in with the end of his walk. His owners had kindly reasoned that there should be no change to Oscar's routine, and that his last hour or so should be a happy one.

Much as I was tempted to make more of a special fuss over him, I tried to ensure the walk went just the way it would ordinarily. I'm quite sure Oscar wouldn't have questioned any special treatment, far less consider the reason behind it, but the normality was as much for my benefit as his. I was feeling emotional enough as it was. And I had another five dogs in my care that required my full attention.

But no matter how hard I tried to remain stoical, I couldn't help but think:

"That's the last time he'll paddle in the river." "That's the last time he'll fetch a stick." "That's the last time he'll pee up against that tree."

Can dogs sense impending death? Can they sense their own death? I don't think Oscar could. Taking him for a walk with his pals that day was most certainly a good move.

I dropped him back at his house, gave him a biscuit treat and a quick cuddle, said 'goodbye' and returned to my van. Sometimes being 'in' on a secret can be difficult. I couldn't hang around in case my emotions transmitted to Oscar.

There were still two small packs to be walked that afternoon. They deserved, and required, my undivided attention.

But it was hard.

I was guilty of clock-watching, knowing the time of Oscar's appointment at the vet. I thought of Oscar and the trust he had always placed in his owners. And me. He would never know, but that trust was well founded. They were doing the right thing. I thought of his owners. How must they be feeling, if I felt this upset?

I sniffed away the odd tear.

Just sometimes, this job sucks.

Life's a bitch. Or, in this case, a dog.

The simple fact is, that since they don't pay taxes, there's only one thing certain in the life of an animal. I don't know though, what is harder to deal with – the pet's passing, or the owner's reaction.

I'm not very good with tears.

When Chicco the cat passed away, it was a double-whammy.

Chicco was a loveable rogue. A ginger tom, he belonged to my sister who also had a similarly coloured, cross-breed dog, Bronte. In general terms, the cat / dog relationship worked well, but that was mainly down to Bronte's gentle, patient and accommodating nature. Chicco definitely ruled the roost, much in the same way as the lasagne-loving cartoon character, Garfield, always wins out over his house-buddy, Odie the dog.

Eventually, however, after many months of trying to minimise their time together, it was decided to re-home Chicco. Although otherwise very good natured, his confidence around Bronte had grown into arrogance. His arrogance developed into bullying and for the ongoing welfare of both pets, a new owner was sought.

I know I shouldn't have any favourites, but Chicco was, after all, my feline nephew. I was as keen as my sister that he went to an experienced cat-lover. And I knew just the lady. A long-established, middle-aged client of mine, she lived locally and on her own. Her previous pet, a rescue cat, had passed away several months earlier.

It was a move that worked well for all parties. I would even be paid for playing and looking after Chicco whenever his new owner was away on business.

Everything was normal for a couple of years. Chicco, possibly the clumsiest cat ever, would charge around the rooms when I visited, like he was on a hot, tin roof. He'd brush against ornaments, picture frames, lamp shades and kitchen utensils. Anything and everything, in fact. I would follow in his wake, swiftly catching, replacing and re-arranging said objects.

To him, this was a simple game of cat and house.

Following a few weeks of not being called upon, I visited Chicco and noticed he had lost weight. I mentioned this to the owner who took him to the vet and a long-term course of medication was prescribed.

Over the next few months, whenever I looked after Chicco, I'd have to pop a couple of tablets down his throat. It was obvious his health was not what it should have been.

Then, as fate would have it, one autumnal Friday evening, his owner had to rush away following a family bereavement. At short notice, I looked in on Chicco. I could tell he was poorly.

The following morning I found him sitting on a window-sill, in a small pool of sick. Although he was purring and not showing any other obvious signs of distress, it was clear the end was approaching. I cleaned him up, and spoon-fed him some slightly warmed, wet cat food which he certainly had the appetite for. Satisfied he was comfortable enough, I left him to rest until my evening visit.

When I called back later though, his condition had deteriorated. Poor soul – he'd managed to get down from the window-sill but had no strength to move anywhere else. Again though, he purred when I picked him up. His temperature had fallen so I sat with him in my arms a while.

Really, he should have gone to the emergency vet. I managed to make contact with his owner whose weekend instantly went from traumatic to unbearable. I could tell she was in bits. She knew Chicco didn't have long to go, but wanted to be with him when he passed away. She knew what would happen if I took him to a vet that evening. It was her intention to leave her family very early the next morning. The drive would take four hours, but she'd be home before lunchtime.

I placed Chicco on the bed, loosely draped a light blanket over him, and left a damp face-cloth within licking distance. He took a little food from my fingers and continued to purr, but already his breathing was shallower than earlier in the day.

It was six in the evening, a Saturday evening, and I was meant to be somewhere else – like viewing my sister's new house just four hundred metres away. Uh oh.

I really couldn't bring myself to tell her about Chicco - certainly not at that particular time, as she and her husband were so excited about getting the keys to their new home. No, it could wait for another day. I prayed Chicco would too.

Having viewed the house, I declined the chance of a few beers, made my excuses and returned to Chicco's house. I spent the next two hours with him, keeping him warm and letting him lick water from my finger-tips. I waited until he fell asleep, checked his breathing and returned home.

I knew what sight would greet me the following morning.

I was right.

I telephoned Chicco's owner who was already on the road towards home. She was tearful as expected. I was close to tears myself as I respected her wish to lay Chicco out on her bed, so that she could take his body to the vet.

I held off telling my sister for a few weeks, choosing my moment carefully one evening when my wife and I had been invited around for a meal. I waited until dessert was being served. I love a good cheesecake, so when my sister burst into tears, and pushed her portion to the side........ well, it would have been rude not to, wouldn't it?

Told you I wasn't good with tears.

*****

14. THE VEHICLE

The biggest asset, in terms of initial outlay for a business such as mine, is the vehicle. It's absolutely imperative that it be both reliable and cost efficient.

I initially opted for a van. Yes, a small, white van. A Citroen Berlingo – with the business logo and contact details displayed along the sides, bonnet and rear doors.

Though I say so myself, it looked the part. It was striking and easily identifiable, but still projected the professional image I was looking for. And as it was being used on the same local roads every day, it soon became such a familiar sight that pedestrians would stop to give a cheery wave as I passed by.

I became a minor, local celebrity. Or at least, that's what I liked to imagine. Postman Pat, the children's television character must have felt like this as he travelled around the fictional village of Greendale in his post van.

For the first six years, the little white van did exactly what was expected of it. It was dependable, efficient, multi-functional, easy to clean and had the added bonus of an excellent sound-system.

I love music. Perhaps I should say I love loud music – all genres, but punk and psychedelic in particular. As soon as the van's ignition key was turned, the music would blare. Sometimes it would be so loud as to prevent me from hearing the engine noise.

I had just completed my daily visit to Bia, the tortoise. He'd awakened from hibernation earlier than expected. I'd let him out his terrarium for a little wander around the kitchen, fed him some fresh greens and ensured he had clean water.

Outside, it was a bright, sunny day. I was ahead of schedule on my rounds. The plan was to get home early, complete my daily business administration, and then relax in the garden with a beer and a book.

I returned to the van, with not a care in the world. I switched on the ignition and was instantly greeted by the summery sound of The Ramones blasting out 'Rockaway Beach.' The track ended as I slipped the gear into reverse and slowly released the clutch.

I did not hear what must have been the desperately intensifying 'bleep, bleep, bleep, bleeeeeeep,' of the van's reverse-sensor.

Fortunately, the Queens punks (that's Queens, the area of New York and not Queen's as in 'by Appointment to Her Royal Highness) stopped to take breath for a couple of seconds as the CD track transitioned to 'Cretin Hop.'

But there was no momentary silence, for the gap was filled with the noise of breaking glass. A lot of breaking glass by the sound of it. I slammed on the brakes and the van jolted to a halt.

I looked in the driver-side wing mirror and saw to my horror that I'd reversed into three large plastic bins. These in turn had violently pushed into what was a tired-looking old wooden shed. Not of sufficient strength to offer any resistance, the shed had surrendered meekly.

The window panes had dropped out so easily it was as if they'd just been waiting for the excuse. The glass had shattered and lay all around the back axel of my van.

The near side of the hut was leaning at a precarious angle, only managing to keep upright by virtue of the fact it was propped up by the more secure far side. The roof remained intact, but was now being worn like a jauntily positioned trilby on a drunk man.

Rather selfishly, my initial fears were for any potential damage to the rear doors of my van. How would I manage my dog-walks tomorrow if the van had to go for repairs?

There was no mark, however, as it had been a slow impact upon the plastic of the bins. The glass from the windows had somehow missed the body of the van and there were no obvious pieces embedded in the tyres. Phew!

The feeling of relief lasted only a few seconds as the enormity of the situation dawned.

I moved the van forward, releasing the pressure on the bins which then returned to their normal position. This movement in turn caused the displaced near panel of the hut to shift further off the perpendicular.

"Please don't let it drop any more. Don't let the roof cave in. Don't let it all collapse like the clichéd pack of cards."

I'm not sure to whom I was praying, or even begging – but if there was indeed a God of Huts, now was the time for him to make his presence felt.

I used the dustpan and brush I carry in the van to sweep up all the glass and deposited it all in one of the bins. I then somehow managed to push, pull, and bang the leaning panel back into position. In doing so, the roof looked to have rearranged itself.

I stood back and took a long, hard look at the resurrected hut. Yeah – it looked good. No different than when I arrived at the house a while earlier. Apart from the lack of windows, of course.

This was a big house, set apart from others in the area and with a huge garden and driveway. I was sure nobody else would have heard the commotion. Perhaps I could just leave. The bins had been emptied since the home-owner had been away. Maybe the bin men would take the rap?

Or maybe I could retrieve the broken glass from the bin and leave it on the driveway beside the hut. I could then leave a couple of rocks lying around so it looked that it was a random act of vandalism.

But should the rocks be placed inside or outside the hut? And how would the glass have fallen? And the village of Kilmacolm is not one normally blighted by such acts. And anyway, why would any self-respecting vandal walk all the way up the long driveway, solely to break two windows in a dilapidated hut?

I've watched enough 'detective' programmes on television to realise that trying to cover one's tracks can only lead to more problems.

No, honesty's the best policy.

I left a note for the owner's return and made a personal call the following day to explain, face to face. I confessed to the broken window panes, but mention of the hut's virtual collapse somehow got stuck between my brain and my mouth. Well, there was no need was there? It was looking good as old and the owner had made no further reference to it.

I offered to pay for the repair to the windows, of course. And it worked. I retained the client.

I returned to the car, my shoulders relaxing to their normal position as I exhaled a massive sigh. I turned the key in the ignition, conscious that the lady was watching me safely negotiate her driveway. The radio sparked to life. Radio6 Music. The volume level had of course been deliberately decreased from 'eleven' to 'one.'

But I could still make out the sweet, soul sounds of Eddie Floyd and 'Knock on Wood.'

While the van escaped any damage in the hut incident, it wasn't so fortunate later in the year. This time, the accident wasn't my fault. Ok, so yes, it was me at the wheel, and it was me who physically reversed the van into another client's garden. But there were mitigating circumstances, so it wasn't just my fault.

It was late morning and the rain that had been falling steadily for the previous three hours had now taken on monsoon proportions. Drops the size of five pence pieces were cascading from the heavens and creating a monumental din as they bounced off the bonnet and roof of the van. I could barely hear my music.

The windows were steamed up, as were the wing mirrors. I was pretty much blind to anything behind me as I reversed the van in past the gateposts and hedge. However, I'd been visiting this house for a couple of years and knew that the driveway was generally clear. And anyway, I'd learned my lesson from past experience and turned the radio off completely so I'd be able to hear the bleeping reverse sensor.

Cruuuunch!

I didn't hear the bleeping reverse sensor. Why? Because it didn't register any warning sound. Not a peep. Or bleep.

I'd reversed the van into a builder's skip that my clients had filled with junk destined for landfill. I moved the van forward and away from the skip, prompting a horrible grating noise as the rear doors of the van prised themselves from the overhanging lip of the skip.

Reversing sensors built into the bumper of conventional vehicles do not, obviously, take into account the design implications of a builder's skip.

Hearing the commotion as he returned to his house from a visit to the shops, an absolutely drenched, elderly neighbour poked his head above the hedge that separates the two properties.

"Oh dear, oh dear, oh dear," he said in what I interpreted as an unintentional BBC TV sitcom voice.

"Did you not see the skip?"

There are times when the diplomacy of silence conveys more than words.

The van was almost five years old. Its impeccable record for reliability was fading somewhat, and weekend visits to my local garage were becoming more and more regular. There was nothing majorly wrong with it, more just a litany of normal wear and tear issues: tyres; brake-shoes; wheel alignment and several other mechanical issues I wouldn't know anything about.

Many men are completely au fait with the workings of cars and vans. Not this one. No siree, Bob. I'm a complete philistine when it comes to motor vehicles and don't mind admitting it. My garage knows this, and could easily take advantage. Yet, they've been exemplary in their service, often attending to my plaintive pleas for assistance when they were already fully booked.

However, I subscribe to the notion that the longer things are going well, so increases the statistical chances of something going wrong. My pessimistic theory was proved correct one lovely Monday morning in spring.

Two days earlier, the van had required some work be done on the brakes. Once again, the garage was most accommodating, fitting the repair into an already busy Saturday morning.

For once though, I wasn't quite so confident that the work had been carried out as diligently as before.

At four o' clock on the Monday morning, I made the regular thirty mile round trip to Glasgow to collect my younger son who was working as a barman. On the return journey, I thought I could hear a slight metallic, grinding noise above the psychedelic metal sound of Japanese band Bo Ningen playing on the sound system.

"Nothing to worry about," I convinced myself, implicitly placing my trust in the garage's work.

A couple of hours sleep and a rushed breakfast later, I drove the eight miles to Paisley for the first dog-walk of the day. The annoying little grinding noise had not magically disappeared while I slept. In fact, it was definitely becoming louder with each mile I travelled. I phoned the garage.

"I really need to bring it in to let you hear this," I said. "It's getting louder and louder by the minute."

I completed the dog-walk and started back towards the garage. By now, the van sounded more like a Boeing 747 and I wondered whether I'd even make it back. I took a back-road, cutting through the countryside to save the embarrassment of driving through suburban streets and drawing attention to myself.

Good call. As I headed down a long and winding slope, startling the sheep and cows as I passed, I felt the steering become difficult. Suddenly, with the steering wheel shuddering violently, the van veered towards the left-hand pavement.

Fifty metres away, and heading in my direction along that very same path was a middle-aged man. Dressed in a short-sleeved shirt and light coloured trousers, he was making the most of the glorious spring morning. If he didn't have a care in the world as he admired the surrounding countryside, he soon would.

Although I was not driving fast, I struggled to control the van. I applied the brakes and tried swerving away from the pavement well in advance of the now distinctly perturbed looking pedestrian.

It's amazing how many things your mind can instantly pick up on in moments of stress.

The walker's expression quickly turned from concern to fright. His gait quickly turned from casual to evasive and I saw him jump over the small wall that separated the pavement from the adjacent field as my van's near-side, rear wheel detached itself from the axel.

Minus one wheel, the van scraped along the road for another thirty or forty metres, slowed by the axel dragging and creating a long score mark on the tarmac. Freed from its shackle, the wheel bounced past the passenger window of the van. I watched as it gathered speed and bounded past the incredulous morning stroller, coming to rest in a distant hedge only when a combination of gravity and traction deprived it of energy.

There were three wheels on my waggon, but unlike in the song, I wasn't 'still rollin' along.'

The van had now come to an unceremonious halt. I could see the pedestrian was laughing, but there was no offer of assistance. I phoned the garage.

"You know that loud grinding noise I was telling you about ….?"

*****

15. THE PACK

(i) The Mix

Television programmes such as 'The Dog Whisperer,' watched with a steaming cup of coffee in one hand and a sticky bun in the other, may lead to us considering ourselves experts in the field of canine behaviour. But nothing prepares you for the first time leading a pack of six excited dogs on their lunchtime walk.

There's plenty to learn, and only one way to do so. It's called 'the hard way.'

Selecting the right mix to comprise the pack is the first hurdle to overcome for any aspiring dog-walker.

As I discovered very quickly, it's difficult to manage a group where there are polar levels of enthusiasm and athleticism. Trying to convince a plodding little Cairn terrier to get his nose out of the undergrowth and at least try to keep up with the playful and energetic labradoodle, is a bit of a non-starter.

Ensuring the dogs are of similar temperament is another issue that needs to be addressed.

Harry, a male, golden Labrador and Jazz, a male, black Labrador are both lovely big docile dogs. I certainly didn't envisage any problems having them both on the same walk. I'd already collected Harry and four other smaller dogs when we arrived at Jazz's house. He lives very close to the park, and so there was no need for him to join the others in the car.

With all six attached to their leads, Jazz on my right hand and Harry on my left, we set off on the short distance to the open parkland. I did notice a couple of glares being exchanged across the heads of the smaller dogs as we walked, but when they were allowed to run free, they just did their own thing and kept a respectful distance from each other.

But as I would grow to learn, generally nothing adverse happens on a walk until The Point of Scheduled Return is reached. All dog-walkers will attest, this is the half-way mark of any walk; the furthest distance from point of set-off.

If there's a sudden, unexpected shower and I don't have my waterproofs with me, this is where the heavens will open. If a dog falls lame or injured, it won't happen until we reach this point. Should I drop a lead from my bag and only notice it's missing when I return to the van, then I know where it's most likely to be found.

And if two dogs, hackles raised, square up to each other like testosterone-fuelled boxers at a pre-fight weigh-in?

It certainly made for an interesting fifteen minute walk back to Jazz's house. Restraining two large dogs that want to kick each other's butt from actually doing so, is not easy. Especially when there are four other smaller dogs that have become excited by the tense atmosphere and want a piece of the action.

The two antagonists are now allotted to different walks and neither has sought to dominate any other dog. As with humans, sometimes individuals are just not compatible. There does not require to be any specific reason. Sometimes it's simply just the mix that's not right.

Having learnt from that incident, I started introducing the dogs to each other before allowing them to walk together. This wasn't a formal type of introduction like you'd read of in a Jane Austen novel – more of a quick sniff and occasional lick, type of acceptance.

I'd bring the new dog to the car and let it greet the others first by sight and then by smell, through the bars of the crate. If there was no indication of an impending slaughter, I'd bring the regular pack members from the car and allow initial contact with the rookie, but at a lead's length. If all looked good, the new dog would be encouraged into the crate before the others, who were always happy to hop in and properly welcome their new friend with open paws.

(ii) The Training

Just about all caring dog owners will consider their pet to be well trained. And most are. But no matter how well they behave with their owners, all dogs walking in my pack must learn the ways of the master. That's me.

However, with the excitement of play and meeting their friends, it's understandable if the collective behaviour doesn't match the standard of the individual.

When they join the pack, each dog must learn the new procedures, like all sitting down quietly before their leads are removed. They must learn new key phrases, like 'time for lead,' for when I want them to have the leads reattached; 'go to the woods,' or 'go to the water,' when I want to send them ahead; 'don't you dare,' when they show any signs of aggression or are thinking of rolling in a smelly dead carcass.

They must also remember a new whistled command, and on some occasions, even respond to a different name. For instance there are two dogs named 'Louis' who walk together. One, the small cockapoo (a cocker spaniel / poodle cross) was generally well behaved and obedient to the call. The other, a young but large, black, flat-coated retriever was both very excitable and a bit of a slow learner. He'd frequently run off to greet other dogs in the park; he'd jump into the fast-flowing river; he'd eat whatever random dog-mess he found; he'd try scrounging biscuits from other passing dog-owners.

He'd just be naughty, full stop. It was his way.

"Louis, no." I'd shout, calmly at first, but with unintentional, increasing exasperation each time I had to repeat myself.

"Louis, come here!"

I'd feel something brush against my leg and looking down, I'd see a very puzzled little cockapoo.

"I'm here, stupid," I'd imagine him saying. "What's up?"

They now each respond to their individual 'Big Louis' and 'Li'l Louis,' monikers.

Of course, a pocket full of biscuits is always going to come in handy for strategic use, but the trouble is, some dogs are just too damned smart.

Buddy, the little white Japanese Spitz, may be young, but he cottons on mighty quickly. The biscuit reward scheme was employed when he was a puppy, and I wanted him to stop mooching around and keep pace with the pack.

After just a couple of half-hour walks, he'd mastered it. For the few days, all was good but then he stopped. I noticed him hanging back, detached from the other five dogs.

"Buddy ..... come on, Buddy," I'd shout while dipping my hand into the biscuit pocket. Within seconds, he was by my side, eagerly looking up and panting expectantly for his reward.

Now, if Buddy's the smart one, then I'm the dim one. It took me two further walks before it dawned he was holding back on purpose in order to receive an otherwise non-forthcoming treat.

You know, I could easily believe he'd be talking to his wee doggie pals behind my back:

"Hey, look you guys. Look, see what I've got this dumb-ass human trained to do."

(iii) The Discipline

Every now and again, their natural exuberance means some dogs require to be reminded how they should behave. Their mischievous behaviour is particularly exasperating for the poor dog-walker. All it takes is for one to step out of line, and the others figure they can do likewise.

Imagine a line of six dogs ranked from quickest to slowest, as they race across a hundred metres of open space to check out the distant female in heat. Picture the bedraggled and harassed dog-walker frantically bringing up the rear. It may look amusing from a bystander's viewpoint but if you're the owner of that poor bitch, then you may just think differently.

This behaviour is understandable. It's the way nature works and no amount of discipline is going to alter that.

But what do you do with a dog that wilfully refuses to come when called? Or one that plays too rough with others? Or jumps into swollen rivers?

I'm probably more guilty than most of humanising the pets I deal with. Most days, they are my only company, and I chat to them as if they are young children.

I find the most successful tactic is to give the errant dog a fatherly lecture. Firmly restrained by its collar, I'll crouch down to eye-level and admonish the miscreant with some stern words. Provided this is done immediately after the dog has stepped out of line, it seems to register. Generally this works well, as all dogs want to please.

Some are slower to learn than others, though. In their case, following a few ineffectual scoldings, they will be placed back on lead for a few days. It soon registers that they are missing out on the fun.

When again allowed to run free, they may misbehave initially, but another five minute stint back on lead, repeated as necessary, works wonders. It eventually clicks and the pack is once again complete and calm.

(iv) The Communication

Dogs are not backward at coming forward. From the tone and delivery of their bark to their body language, they are quick to let me know what they want or how they're feeling.

Marley, the large springer spaniel, will turn to me at the point on our walk where the woodland path forks.

"Which way?" he seems to say as he pants enthusiastically, his tongue lolling out the corner of his mouth and his tail wildly flapping.

"To the water," I'll say.

Marley will bounce up and down and though not normally one for directly socialising with the others, he'll run up to them:

"We're going in the water. The water. Come on – we're going to the water!"

And then he'll be gone, leaving those less enthusiastic in his whirlwind wake. To the water.

Rowan is another brown and white springer. Smaller in stature than Marley, and at eleven years of age, he's some four years older. But age is no barrier to playtime – even if his eyesight and hearing is failing to the extent that I often have to retrieve the sticks I throw for him.

Every day, on our regular route, we'd pass a woodland clearing. This is the place he associated with fetching the stick. Or, more accurately, losing the stick. Unfortunately though, for a period of several months, the area was sealed off for tree-felling.

Poor Rowan – whenever we approached, he'd race off ahead of me and stand at the corner of the lane that would lead into the clearing. He'd bounce up and down on his hind legs, eyes sparkling with anticipation.

"Can we? Can we? Please? Oh, come on. Please?"

When I pass by with Oscar, his younger springer housemate, Rowan's head drops, the wagging tail slows, eventually resting between his hind legs, and he reluctantly traipses along behind us.

"Tomorrow? Please? Yeah – tomorrow. Yeah?"

Whatever their emotion, it's the eyes that let me know how the dogs are feeling. Murphy, the little black Jack Russell flashes a cheeky glint before he tries to mount a dog over twice his size. Ozzie, a bearded collie, casts his sad eyes downward when he follows me to the front door as I prepare to leave for my next walk. And Jazz, the normally stoical black Labrador, exudes undiluted pride in his eyes as he repeatedly taps my leg with his snout to show me he's somehow managed to steal the tennis ball from Marley.

But rather worryingly, I have also evidenced fear being reflected in a dog's eyes. Only once, but the memory of that instance remains with me today.

Dexter was a lovely old golden retriever. I had been told by his owner that he could be a little unpredictable around younger dogs, but for two years of walking with him, I had seen no evidence of this.

It had to happen, though. Out on the local cycle track one icy winter's morning, we approached a young dog. We saw this pup most mornings. The two dogs would always greet each other in the accustomed manner and walk on their separate ways.

This day was different for some reason, and Dexter launched himself at the puppy. It was no quick skirmish of bluster and bluff – it was all out, fur-flying savagery. The other dog's owners stood rooted in horror. I jumped in, and after slipping on the ice – and cracking a rib in the process – I parted the two, though not before receiving a nasty, accidental bite to my hand.

Dexter's adversary and its owners scurried away after a cursory mention of:

"Oh – your hand is bleeding. Are you all right?"

"What do you bloody think?" I thought to myself as my blood dripped onto the track and a searing pain pierced through my ribcage.

I crouched down, face to face with Dexter.

"Oh Dexter! You BAD dog."

At the mention of 'bad,' poor Dexter visibly flinched and I saw that fear in his eyes. He didn't struggle to get away from my grasp, but instead, quickly lay down and rolled over and cowered in submission.

Dexter was terrified. Without exception, every other dog I had dealt with in a similar manner would simply shake off the rebuke and walk on.

I was shocked and, I don't mind adding, a little upset. I got the distinct impression that he'd been subjected to some form of physical punishment in the past.

Arriving back at his house, I noticed his owner's car in the driveway. Should I mention the incident and Dexter's reaction? I was faced with a bit of a quandary. I couldn't really cast aspersions in the face of my client. They'd be most offended if I incorrectly implied they were mistreating the dog.

On the other hand, if there was anything untoward going on, maybe it would stop if the client got the impression that I knew.

Anyway – all mental debate vanished as soon as I entered the house.

"Look at your hand! Are you OK? What happened?"

Without pausing for thought, and perhaps fuelled by the adrenalin still coursing through my body, I just blurted out the circumstances and my concerns. I'm sure I didn't actually make any specific accusations, but the owner certainly read between the lines.

"Oh no. I can't understand why he'd do that. He's never been mistreated. Never. No."

The lady doth protest too much, I considered. But what else was she going to say?

Two weeks later, my services were dispensed with. Dexter now has another dog-walker.

(v) The Young

When a puppy joins the pack, there is great excitement. The older dogs react very much like humans do when a new mother brings her baby into her place of work. Except, they're not big on baby showers.

Everything stops for a few moments while the bewildered pup is enthusiastically prodded and sniffed to within an inch of its young life.

And that's it. There's no time for standing on ceremony. There's more important things that older dogs need to do on a walk. Scents need to be sprayed; birds need to be chased; smelly stuff needs to be found for rolling in.

Thankfully, one dog often takes more of an interest than others ....

"OK kidder – you're in. Now tag onto the back and try to keep up. That guy over there with the glasses? He thinks he's the leader. Best for all we allow him to think that. If you get the chance, there's usually some fresh fox-scat over by the entrance to that field. Stay away from the water until you've grown a bit. Oh – and I wouldn't bother trying to take the tennis ball from Marley. We run a tight group here. Don't do anything to upset the balance and you'll be just fine."

Angus, a big golden retriever, would happily take on this role. He'd be more patient with the little ones than most. He'd lie on his back and allow the new puppies to climb all over him. Some would mischievously bite his back legs as he tried to walk away, but he never once snapped back.

The pups generally go through three stages of development – a bit like young children, although I'm no paediatrician and this is simply a basic observation.

Firstly, they are full of wonderment at this new world they've been thrust into. They are cute and so very much dependent on you, as their surrogate leader.

Then, after a few walks to settle into the pack, they tend to become a little more adventurous and explorative. They are still a tad unsure of many things. However, they're desperate to please and do all they can, like respond to basic commands and whistles, in order to ingratiate themselves.

Finally, after a couple of months, they reckon they know it all. They become cocky. They become brattish even. They ignore the whistles and commands. They start to pester the older dogs and the dynamics of the pack are shifted from the norm.

Call for Callie!

Callie, a chocolate brown, short-haired German pointer was a godsend. She was one of the first dogs I recruited and at only ten months old was still in the puppy phase herself. But over the course of the four years walking together, we build up such a strong rapport that she became my unofficial pack lieutenant.

Although I often referred to her as my 'Enforcer,' she was like a kindly but strict school ma'am to the other dogs, especially the new ones.

Should Callie hear me speaking sternly to a 'phase three' puppy, she'd join in.

"Yap. Yap. Ok – that's enough. If you're joining this pack, you better get your tail in gear. Come on – behave"

Similarly, if there were any persistent stragglers, I could send her back:

"Callie – go get Mac. Go get him." I'd point in the direction of the tardy little Westie, and off she'd go.

Of course, the puppies do eventually fall in with the pack. It may take the odd nip from older, less patient dogs. It may take a few days of being deprived of treats when all others receive theirs. It may also mean them walking on-lead for a prolonged period.

But eventually the penny drops and very often the owner will comment on how much better behaved their pet is within the pack than when they walk them alone.

(vi) The Elderly

In the eight years I've been running the petcare business, I've noticed my energy levels diminish and any niggling little injuries take much longer to clear. Old age doesn't come alone, I'm told.

The dogs in the pack are no different. Some have been with me from the start, and they weren't young pups even then.

But rather like myself, the dogs don't seem to acknowledge the age process. They still love the thought of chasing after a ball or each other. In some cases though, it definitely is a case of the mind being willing, but the body being weak.

Sam and Gem are from the same household. Sam is a tubby little Cairn terrier and Gem, a loveable Staffordshire bull terrier. Both are around ten years old.

Sam has never been one for expending any unnecessary energy. He's a very sociable dog, preferring to spend most of his walks checking every clump of grass for the scent of any dog that passed the same way. Or, just as likely, he's trying to find that elusive McDonald's wrapper with some left-over scraps stuck in the seam. He likes his food, does Sam.

He wasn't exactly built for speed, so the aging process hasn't noticeably slowed him down. It's his eyesight that's been affected by age. He now walks on-lead following several episodes of bumping into branches of trees and falling into streams.

Despite the sometimes fearsome reputation accredited to her breed, Gem is adorable. All she wants to do in life is chase thrown balls. She would be so committed in her pursuit that after she'd caught the ball, momentum would force her into a couple of uncontrolled somersaults. Nothing got in her way. If there was an obstruction between her and the ball, like a bush, she'd simply charge through it.

I was always careful not to throw a ball anywhere near a fence or a wall.

Gradually though, from around the age of nine, her stamina started to wane. She'd stop playing after three-quarters of the walk, then a half of the walk, then a quarter.

Nowadays, she jumps out the car full of enthusiasm, ears pricked, eyes dilated and runs about twenty metres with short staccato steps, before allowing one of the other dogs to retrieve the ball.

She'll then walk close by me, snuggling into my legs when the weather's inclement, her tail curled up between her legs, her greying muzzle carried low. It's hard not to feel sorry for her.

Mrs Lang was not one of the pack. She did like her biscuits (she'd often offer me a digestive) but I doubt she'd have been able to keep up with the others on our walks.

I walked her friendly little West Highland terrier, Ailsa. Just once every fortnight. I think it was the dog's treat when the old lady's meagre pension came through.

When I first met her, Mrs Lang would have been in her early eighties, still quite a fit lady with a sharp mind. She liked to talk but had no direct family in Scotland and I suspect didn't have many visitors or went out the house much.

I became her soundboard, though I could be unkind and spell that differently. She would regale me with tales of when she and her now deceased husband had emigrated to Canada.

Gradually though, I could sense age catching up with her. She became slow to answer the door, would forget where she'd hidden the money to keep it safe, and she'd repeat the same story over and over.

As time passed, her condition deteriorated. Some days she'd shout that she'd already paid me; sometimes she wouldn't get out of bed and I'd spend ages trying to rouse her by phone calls. One day she came to the door and couldn't remember who I was. She grew more confused and agitated by the week.

I was, however, able to see Ailsa was still being looked after. But I decided I could no longer take money from her owner, and some other arrangement would have to be made.

It's difficult to know where checking on somebody's well-being becomes interference but I knew I had to try to do something.

After some thought, I decided to contact the vet's surgery where I had, on occasion, taken Ailsa to be treated for a skin condition. I told the vets of my concerns and asked that if they had any family contacts on file, to please ask them to phone me.

A few days later, I received a call from a niece in the South of England. Having explained the situation to her, she said she'd come up as soon as she could, and take things from there.

After a couple of weeks, I received a lovely 'thank you' card from the niece who explained that she'd managed to find a suitable care home for Mrs Lang, and that Ailsa had been successfully re-homed.

I felt a little guilty and sad at the result of my action, but knew in my heart it was the right thing to do.

Heck – my job had just developed social service wings.

(vii) The Habits

It amuses me to see the habits formed by dogs within the pack, and how they seem to respect each other's. Even Marley's daily, angry rant at other pack members jumping into the crate with him, is accepted as the norm by most. They all just give me a look that says:

"Good grief ... here we go again. What 's his problem?" and pile in.

Well – Big Louis, the flat coated retriever is the exception.

"Go on Louis, jump up," I'd say every day for the first three months.

From the vacant look on his face, I may as well have asked him to solve a Rubik cube puzzle. He's now two years old, and has almost got it – his developed habit is to stand half in, half out of the crate and wait for me to gently push him in.

Others, like the two springers Oscar and Rowan, have developed a more organised habit. When I collect them from their home, they both run out to the car, and whoever gets to it first, jumps straight in. The other follows. They will then ensure that Oscar sits to the right hand side of the crate and Rowan to the left.

After the walk, I bring them both back to the car together, Oscar who is the younger yet more dominant dog, will without fail respectfully wait for Rowan to hop in first, after which they will shuffle around so each sits on the correct side. No amount of coaxing will alter this routine.

The lunchtime pack of six dogs even organise themselves in advance of their drop-off point. After the first dog has been returned home, the remaining five will somehow sort themselves so that the next to get out will be closest to the door.

Sadie, a toy poodle, will always try to pick up, and swallow, any little stones she sees before starting the walk. Molly the Jack Russell, will instantly roll over when I call to collect her. If I don't tickle her tummy and chin, I either have to pick her up and carry her, or slide her out the house on her back.

Others have the more questionable habit of coprophagia – eating other dogs' or animals' poo. Or some, like Harry the golden Labrador and now his housemate, Buddy the Japanese spitz, have a severe grass habit. Harry in particular will run ahead of the pack to eat as much as he can, knowing that when I catch up, he will be forced to move on.

The ingestion of the grass is less objectionable than the swallowing of other dogs' poo. However, the other end of the process is infinitely more disgusting. I am frequently witness to a partially constipated and distressed dog running around with what looks like a long, horse's tail attached to its backside. The dogs in question are more than relieved to receive a helping (plastic bag covered) hand with its removal.

The joys of being a Pet Professional.

*****

16. THE FRIENDSHIPS

All dog owners will readily acknowledge the strong bond that develops between them and their pet. What I didn't expect, was that a similarly strong friendship would be forged between the dogs and myself. Even with those like Benji the boxer, who are exercised on their own, and just once a week.

I have visited and walked Benji since he was a tiny puppy, small enough to be held in one hand. He is now six years old and at head height, comes up to my waist. He is the biggest and strongest dog I care for.

But he's also one of the gentlest and each morning I arrive, by way of greeting me, he goes straight to his toy box and brings me something from it. He doesn't look to play or wrestle over it. He simply gives it to me.

Rowan, the elderly springer, may be losing the knack of retrieving sticks and balls that are thrown for him, but anything he does find of interest on our walk, is to be shared with me. Normally this is just a discarded plastic bottle. Once it was a shoe. In the middle of nowhere and down a deserted country lane. No, I don't know either.

He's always so pleased with himself when he drops the gift that it was hard to know how to react when, as darkness fell on a late autumnal walk, he presented me with a cloven hoof. A reasonably fresh one too.

I hated the thought of a dead deer being scavenged upon not far from where I stood.

But after a moment's reflection I began to sincerely hope that indeed was the case. As I stood alone in the enveloping gloom, with only two dogs and my overactive imagination for company, a dark, alternative thought raced through my mind.

There could be Hell to pay for this.

"Rowan. Oscar. Time for leads. We're going home."

The extent of that canine / human friendship has surprised me on a couple of occasions in particular.

I first met Poppy, another toy poodle, when she was just two months old and started walking with her a few weeks later. She was delightful. And well behaved. The two don't always go together.

She was on my books for only six months before her owner's shift work patterns changed and my services were no longer required. I didn't see Poppy at all in the following nine months or so. Then, one day, after I'd returned the last of the lunchtime pack back to their home, Poppy passed on the opposite side of the road with her owner.

I cast a casual glance, but it didn't dawn on me who she was. Poppy though had no doubts. She yelped and yelped, then ran straight across the road, jumped up at me and licked my face as I stooped to greet her.

It's now three years on from that day and although she has never again joined the pack for a walk, she still runs to me should we be in the park at the same time.

Saphie the ultra-bouncy labradoodle went one better.

Again, I'd been walking her since she was old enough to mix with other dogs. We'd walk a mile or so along the country cycle track that links her village with mine, before returning along the route we came. This we did for over three years until, as with Poppy, her owners' circumstances changed.

About seven months after my last walk with her, I met Saphie and her owner while I was walking another couple of dogs on the same stretch of cycle track. Saphie recognised me from some distance away and bounded up. The natural, smiling look on a labradoodle's face was positively beaming as she ignored the other dogs completely and jumped around me yelping with excitement.

I chatted with her owner for a few minutes and gave Saphie a couple of biscuits. She eventually had a good sniff around the two dogs that were with me and then her owner hooked her onto a lead and they headed off in the opposite direction to us.

Over five minutes later, having passed the one mile point, we were about to turn around and head back when I heard a heavy panting noise behind me. Before I could turn to see what was approaching, two large, curly-haired paws slammed into my back.

It was Saphie.

She was all over me again, and it took a good few minutes to calm her down enough to hook her onto a spare lead and walk her back along to track towards home. Several minutes later, I could make out in the distance what looked like a middle-aged woman, hands on knees, struggling for breath

It was indeed Saphie's owner.

On nearing home, she had figured it would be safe to let Saphie back off-lead. But Saphie wasn't going to let such an opportunity pass, and immediately took off back down the cycle track, ignoring her owner's desperate shouts for her return. She had kept running, for well over half a mile, until she found me.

We all walked together, back to the house. Saphie had calmed down by now, but her demeanour had changed from ecstatic to sad.

"Bye Saphie," I said. "See you."

I tried to keep my tone upbeat. Saphie's tail wagged, but slowly. She put on a brave face, accepting the inevitability of parting.

Our paths have not crossed since.

*****

17. THE CUTE

I sometimes feel a little guilty, charging my clients to look after their newly acquired puppies and kittens. My previous life as a Bank Manager never involved this much fun. But coming from a financial background, monetary guilt is something I've learned to live with. It soon fades, come pay day.

And anyway, young pets are generally pretty hard work. They may look all sweetness and light, but they are the embodiment of devilment. Kittens especially.

Never has a young cat been more aptly named. Rambo, a tiny little brown and black striped tabby, and his sister, Poppy, had arrived early.

"We've timed this all wrong, I know," said their owner. "We hadn't expected to get the kittens until after we returned from holiday next week. But they'll be all right with the run of the hallway and all upstairs, won't they?"

"Should be fine," I said.

I knew the house well as I'd also been regularly looking after Millie, their six-year old ginger, black and white cat since she herself was a kitten.

"But, can you make sure that Millie stays in the kitchen, please? She's not very tolerant of the wee ones just yet. We really need to keep them apart for now, but she'll still have access to the garden through the cat flap. Rambo and Poppy are too young to be inoculated, so they can't go outside – another reason they can't be allowed into the kitchen."

"Yeah, that's fine, no worries" I replied.

How wrong could I be?

My first visit to the kittens was eight hours after the owners departed on holiday. As I turned the key in the glass-fronted front door, I could see down the hallway to the kitchen. The door was ajar. I remembered it wasn't a latch door, just one of those than can be gently pushed shut. And open.

The owners had seemingly misjudged the strength, intelligence and inquisitiveness of these kittens.

I called out for them, but they were nowhere to be seen. Neither was the older cat for that matter, but that didn't surprise me. She loved to be outdoors and only appeared when she was hungry. I walked upstairs. All doors were closed.

The house sat back from what can at times be a busy road, and the owners had already lost Millie's brother, Fidget, to a speeding car. My mind raced through all sort of terrible scenarios as I started down the stairs. Had the kittens, once in the kitchen, managed to scramble through the cat flap? Would they still be in the garden, or would they have wandered onto the bordering golf course? Would they be able to find their way back? Or worse – maybe they'd wandered onto the road? Oh God. Please, no.

Then, just as I passed one of the closed bedroom doors, I heard a very faint little mew. Then again.

Puzzled, but relieved, I pushed open the door and two very hungry little kittens charged past my feet and headed straight for the room in which their food had been placed.

It seems all doors within the house had been fitted with the same 'push' mechanism as the kitchen. The little rascals had managed to prise the door sufficiently open to enter the room, but the tight hinges had forced it closed behind them.

It was a young boy's room with a full drum kit installed in one corner while rock-star posters and football banners adorned the walls. It wasn't the tidiest, as you'd expect of a young lad.

There was a rather obvious smell emanating from somewhere amongst the chaos.

I quickly identified its source and lifted the offending solids from the floor. I could also see a wet patch on the carpet, so that was attacked with the disinfectant I carry in my car.

I finished my usual cat-visit duties and played a while with the little darlings. Who wouldn't?

Realising Poppy, and especially Rambo, had discovered the hidden delights of the kitchen, (Millie's food) it was only a matter of time before they did try pushing open the cat-flap and venturing outside as I'd initially feared. And of course, I didn't want a repeat of them using one of the bedrooms as a gigantic litter tray.

Using all the school bags, wellington boots, kitchen stools, litter bins, in fact anything I could easily move around the house, I barricaded all the doors and hoped for the best.

That foxed them. The rest of the week passed without further incident.

However, the weather was unusually hot for Scotland that week. Intensely hot. Three days after Rambo and Poppy's excellent adventure, a nauseating stench permeated the house. I tracked it back to the room in which the little rascals had been entrapped.

There was nothing else for it. I had to rummage.

A couple more, now dried out, patches of urine soaked carpet required to be zapped with disinfectant and soapy water. But there was still an overriding stomach churning smell in the air. It took a few minutes, but finally I found the source.

Drummers often place old bed-sheets, duvets and rags within the large kick drum to muffle the sound. Guess what I found amongst the pile?

I didn't charge for laundry services.

A few weeks later, with the kittens still to be inoculated before being allowed outside, I was asked to look after Millie, Rambo and Poppy for another spell. This time the family had prepared for all eventualities.

The kitchen door was only able to be opened by lifting a heavy chain from a hook that had been drilled into the door frame. Not even the most inventive of kittens can do that.

The precautions upstairs were even more imposing. An array of brightly coloured climbing ropes, attached in a criss-cross arrangement to each of the bedroom door handles, gave the appearance of infrared laser beams.

An accomplished cat burglar would find it difficult to sneak into the bedrooms this week.

*****

18. THE UNEXPECTED

I may not evidence much in the way of the 'thoroughly modern intellect,' as suggested by Oscar Wilde, but one thing I've learnt from this petcare business, is to 'expect the unexpected.'

If my diary is full of walks for the day, I expect cancelations; if there's money in the Business bank account, I expect an expensive fault to develop in the car and if it's a lovely, hot sunny morning, then I expect rain in the afternoon.

I know. I'm a kind of 'glass half-empty' type of guy. But this is West of Scotland. That's how we roll.

It's one thing though, expecting the unexpected, but the real trick would be an ability to predict just what the 'unexpected' would entail. But then, I guess that would simply make it the 'expected.'

It would certainly have been of benefit to know what lay around the corner the day I walked with Rocky and Lady, two elderly and related cross-breeds.

For a change, I decided to take them along a country road, normally devoid of traffic so they could mooch around, off lead, in the hedgerows and borders. There were so many interesting smells to be investigated and they were totally engrossed.

We had almost reached The Point of Scheduled Return when, in complete unison, they stopped in their tracks. Four ears immediately faced forward. Something was coming our way.

I brought their leads out from my bag, thinking perhaps a car or a tractor was about to appear over the brow of the hill fifty metres away. Unusually, I didn't have to call Rocky and Lady over to me. They were already by my side, tails between their legs, ears now alternating between erect and forward-facing, and laid tightly back against their heads.

They would not take one more forward step. They were rooted to the spot, terrified.

The cause of their fear quickly became apparent.

Silently at first, a pack of forty foxhounds appeared. They were from the hunt kennels in the village and were out for morning exercise. As they rapidly advanced towards us, they noticed the presence of Rocky and Lady.

These were pure hunt dogs, not bred for their social skills. Their tails were erect, and wavering with excitement, their barks rasping and rather unfriendly. The lead dog broke into a canter, headed in our direction. Others quickly followed.

I was rather surprised at just how tall and muscular these dogs stand. The standard height is around two feet, but they seemed considerably more. Perhaps my apprehension exaggerated the fact. Whatever, I didn't fancy taking precise measurements.

The hunt master, sat high on his white horse, was having a job keeping them all together and in check. Fortunately, there were two assistants on foot. They cracked their whips, shouted a couple of expletive embellished commands, and brought the breakaways back into the pack, thus preventing my two becoming fresh dog meat.

The last foxhound in the pack had slowed, detaching itself slightly from the others. It passed by, but after about ten metres, it turned its head back towards us.

"Next time, my friends. Next time. We know where you live," it said in a husky, whispered and threatening manner, before breaking into a manic, evil sounding, canine laugh. Maybe.

My heart was pounding and my imagination racing. Rocky and Lady were trembling. After a few minutes to settle ourselves, and let the pack disappear into the distance, we turned back towards the village.

Not once did the two dogs waste any time checking out the scents left by the pack. I had never seen them so keen to head home.

I would have never envisioned a seemingly straightforward visit to a tortoise resulting in anything unexpected.

And yet, just a few weeks after almost demolishing the client's garden hut, itself not exactly an expected occurrence, I found myself in a rather surprising position.

I'd finished the last of my scheduled visits to Bia and was to post the house keys back through the client's letterbox. It was the type of letterbox I imagine postmen despising, being only a few inches above the foot of the door. For security reasons, I'd been requested to throw the keys as far into the house as I could.

I did as asked, but without noticing my van key had snagged itself onto the client's key-ring. I managed to skid all the keys along the parquet flooring in the hallway, with them coming to rest about three feet away.

I returned to the van and patted my pockets in search of the key. I found a couple of broken dog biscuits; a few poo bags, empty of course; three pounds sixty-three in coins, and two Rowntrees Fruit Pastilles. I'd forgotten about them. I'd save them for the drive home – or the bus or taxi ride as were now looking the more likely options.

As if a slow motion replay, my mind reviewed the actions of the past few moments. Gradually, the reality of the situation dawned.

What a klutz.

I had a duplicate key, yes. But it was in a kitchen drawer at home, some eight miles away.

I could phone home and arrange someone to bring it to me. Or maybe I should call a taxi and go home for it myself. Except, my phone was in the locked van.

I was stranded. I didn't think my day could get any worse, but Fate is not one to play by the rules, and is not averse to kicking a man when he's down. A man wearing glasses, at that.

There was nothing else for it. I got down on all fours, rolled up the sleeve of my fleece, pushed my right arm through the letterbox and fumbled around in the forlorn hope of grabbing the car key. Fortunately, I could lay flat enough on the ground to peer through the letterbox at the same time. Agonisingly, I could see that my outstretched fingertips were still a good six inches short of their target.

I pulled my arm back through the letterbox, scraping it on the metal frame in doing so. I then searched around the garden for an appropriately formed twig. It had to be about eight to ten inches long, with a bent or hooked end. It had to be clean enough not to leave marks or dirt on the owner's floor, and sturdy enough not to break and leave tell-tale signs of some strange happenings.

The perfect specimen found, I tried again to hook the van key via the letterbox.

In my younger days, I never was much good in the amusement arcades, when it came to grabbing a teddy bear or a stick of rock with that automated crane contraption. It was quickly apparent my ineptitude remained.

From my prone position, I stretched, fumbled, twisted, prodded, cursed and then cursed again. To make matters worse, a dirty great big black cloud hovered overhead and threatened to add to my misery.

I hadn't realised just how much one can actually hate an inanimate object.

After many minutes, I finally managed to slip the twig under the small ring that was attached to the key. All I then had to do was carefully drag it to me and lift it the six inches from the floor to the letterbox, then pull it through.

Easy.

Not so. All that movement through the little gap afforded by the letterbox had resulted in my hand and arm becoming swollen. I couldn't pull them back through. I was stuck.

And the owner would be returning in an hour or so.

With the benefit of hindsight, it was easy to consider the better option would have been to camp out on the doorstep, wait for her return and explain what had happened. I'd reasoned however, that, on top of almost knocking down the hut on that earlier visit, my reputation for running a slick and efficient business could be somewhat tarnished.

But compared to the owner discovering my legs protruding from the house entrance and my arm rammed through the letterbox up to my shoulder, perhaps it would have proved a more rational decision.

"Keep calm," I told myself. "Don't panic."

I lay there quietly for a minute or two. I tried to gently pull my arm once again. Nothing. Nothing other than pain, that is.

Then it hit me – that 'eureka' moment. In my commando shorts, I carried a small tube of Factor 30 sun cream. The summer sun in the West of Scotland is not predictable like on the continent, or even Southern England for that matter. As a fair-skinned Scot working outdoors though, I like to be prepared.

I shifted position as best I could and with my free hand, struggled to retrieve the cream. Having popped the top open, it was then the not so simple task of smearing some onto the trapped arm.

Duly lubricated, I tentatively extricated my arm, and car key, from the Venus fly-trap of a letterbox. Already, the bruising was apparent. I was also discovering just how much sunblock stings when applied to broken, scraped skin.

I used my fleece to wipe the metal surroundings clear of any residual cream and returned to my van.

I started the engine and paying careful attention to avoiding the bloody garden hut, I raced out the driveway, down to the main road and headed home.

I may never play the piano again, but at least I'd managed to preserve my professional reputation.

Until, of course, I wrote this chapter.

*****

19. THE REFLECTION

It's now eight years since I started this petcare business, and despite what the Jack Russell's owner told me on that very first dog walk, every day still brings a degree of madness. Which is a good thing. Without it, this relatively short book would have been a mere pamphlet.

Stemming from my schooldays, it's been an interesting set of events and circumstances that have led me to writing this piece. Had I been any good at maths and physics, none of this would have happened. I twice failed the Higher qualification for both subjects, so that was an early end of my plan to study either dentistry or accounting at University. A narrow escape, perhaps?

Had I passed those exams, I wouldn't have joined the Bank of Scotland straight from school, and so wouldn't have been made redundant some twenty-eight years later. And if I hadn't been made redundant, I wouldn't have invested any funds and trust in my so-called 'friend,' and his business. I would have been blissfully unaware of what kind of person he really is.

Had he not condemned me to my second redundancy, I wouldn't have experienced the pain of ten months job hunting. Neither would I have been so desperate for work that I was forced to start my own small business.

Everything happens for a reason, though. Maybe it was simply meant to be.

I don't dwell on the question though. I'm far too shallow and impatient for all that.

What matters is, all those potentially fateful circumstances have resulted in positives. I enjoy my work. I appreciate the hours spent walking in the fresh air. I love the company I keep throughout the working day, and I'm excited by the variety of situations I often find myself in.

Many people are stuck behind their desks in a stuffy offices, being leant upon by bosses who are only interested is exceeding nonsensical targets, massaging their egos and furthering their careers. I, on the other hand, am to be found in the vibrant and beautiful, leafy lanes of Renfrewshire, Scotland.

I'll be crawling through chicken runs; cleaning out rabbit hutches; administering medication to small pets; walking dogs in the rain and cleaning out cat litter trays.

I'll be dressed in my green polo shirt and green shorts, with green wellington boots slapping against my naked calves. I'll likely have numerous midges and flies entrapped in my short Mohawk hairstyle, and smell of damp dogs and rabbit wee, but I wouldn't have it any other way.

Form an orderly queue, ladies.

THE END

*****

ABOUT THE AUTHOR

Cee Tee (Colin) Jackson is an ex-bank manager, now running his own small petcare / dog-walking business in the west of Scotland.

A bit of a short-arse, with a short attention span, it's no surprise that this, his first book, is also on the short side.

Other than family, work and writing, his passions are music and sport. For many years he ran his Loud Horizon music blog in addition to writing for Artrocker magazine. Having competed at several sports, including athletics, soccer, baseball and tennis, injuries and age are now catching up, although he still enjoys circuit training sessions three times a week.

Cee Tee is married to wife Diane and they have two grown sons, Greig and Brett.

_____

www.ceeteejackson.com

https://twitter.com/Ceeteejackson

https://www.facebook.com/pages/Cee-Tee-Jackson/933137280065794

Printed in Poland
by Amazon Fulfillment
Poland Sp. z o.o., Wrocław